Interior of the keep at Canterbury

THE CASTLES
OF KENT

Mike Salter

FOLLY PUBLICATIONS

ACKNOWLEDGEMENTS

The photographs in this book were taken by the author between 1983 and 2000 except for those of Allington taken by Paul Remfry. The old prints and postcards are reproduced from originals in the author's collection. The author also drew the plans, many of which are on a common scale of 1:800, although a few buildings are shown at 1:400 and large buildings and earthworks are generally at 1:2000.

AUTHOR'S NOTES

This series of books (see full list inside the back cover) are intended as portable field guides giving as much information and illustrative material as possible in volumes of modest size, weight and price. As a whole the series aims to make information available about less well known buildings. The aim in the castle books has been to mention, where the information is known to the author, owners or custodians of buildings who erected or altered parts of them, and those who were the first or last of a line to hold an estate, an important office, or a title. Those in occupation at the time of dramatic events such as sieges are also often named. Other owners and occupants whose lives had little effect on the condition of the buildings are generally not mentioned, or ghost stories, myths and legends.

The books are intended to be used in conjunction with the Ordnance Survey 1:50,000 scale maps. Grid references are given in the gazetteers together with a coded system indicating which buildings can be visited or easily seen by the public from adjacent open spaces which is explained on page 16. Generally speaking, maps will be required to find some of the lesser known earthworks and moated houses.

Each level of a building is called a storey in this book, the basement being the first storey with its floor near courtyard level unless specifically mentioned as otherwise.

Measurements given in the text and scales on the plans are in metres, the unit used by the author for all measurements taken on site. Although the buildings were designed using feet the metric scales are much easier to use and are now standard amongst academics working on historic buildings and ancient sites. For those who feel a need to make a conversion 3 metres is almost 10 feet. Unless specifically mentioned as otherwise all dimensions are external at or near ground level, but above the plinth if there is one. On the plans the original work is shown black, post 1800 work is stippled and alterations and additions of intermediate periods are hatched.

ABOUT THE AUTHOR

Mike Salter is 47 and has been a professional writer and publisher since he went on the Government Enterprise Allowance Scheme for unemployed people in 1988. He is particularly interested in the planning and layout of medieval buildings and has a huge collection of plans of churches and castles he has measured during tours (mostly by bicycle and motorcycle) throughout all parts of the British Isles since 1968. Wolverhampton born and bred, Mike now lives in an old cottage beside the Malvern Hills. His other interests include walking, maps, railways, board games, morris dancing, playing percussion instruments and calling dances with a folk group.

Tower on city walls of Canterbury

CONTENTS

Inside the front cover is a map of buildings described in this book.

INTRODUCTION

The type of defensible residence known to the Normans as a castle was introduced to England after Duke William of Normandy defeated King Harold at Hastings in 1066 and took the English Crown. He granted estates to his followers in return for specified periods of military service. The Norman lords or barons then in turn gave units of land called manors to their knights, again in return for military service, this system being known as feudalism. The thin veneer of land-owning Normans consolidated their fragile hold on the land by constructing castles serving as residences, strongholds and status symbols. The Romans and Saxons built purely military forts and defences around settlements but the Normans introduced the idea of powerful individuals erecting fortresses to serve as their private residences and as the administrative centres of their manors. The Domesday Book of 1086 records several royal and baronial castles in Kent as having been built by then. These castles were initially not of mortared stone but of earth and wood, which allowed rapid construction.

These early castles often had a high mound raised from material taken out of the surrounding ditch and having on top the lord's residence in the form of a two or three storey timber tower surrounded by a palisade. The mound summit was reached by a ramp up from a forecourt or bailey in which were sited a range of stores, workshops, a hall and other apartments, and a chapel, all originally built of wood. Sometimes the mound took an alternative form called a ringwork with a high rampart surrounding the lord's house, and the greater castles usually had an additional outer bailey beyond the main entrance. Castles of these types continued to be built for over a century after the Norman conquest and can only be precisely dated when there is a historical record of their foundation or good archaeological evidence.

Bailey of Caesar's Camp, Folkestone

St Leonard's Tower, West Malling

For the first two generations after Duke William's invasion of 1066 masons were in short supply compared with carpenters and labourers, partly because the Saxons and Danes mostly erected buildings of wood except for important churches. Buildings of mortared stone took several years of comparatively peaceful conditions to construct. Fortifications would have been vulnerable to attack during long periods when foundations were being laid in deep trenches, so wooden structures raised on timber posts were seen as an easier option when defences were required in a hurry, as in the eight days that Duke William spent on strengthening an existing fortress (probably more in the nature of a fortified town) at Dover immediately after his victory over the Saxons at Hastings. Slight traces of his work there have been found by excavation. Timber eventually rots when in contact with damp earth so when more peaceful conditions allowed, wooden structures were gradually replaced by buildings of stone. At Rochester a wooden castle built by William I just outside the Roman city walls was replaced in 1088 on the orders of William II (Rufus) by a castle with a stone curtain wall located further north, within a corner of the Roman wall. Considerable portions of it still remain. Also probably of the last years of the 11th century is the enigmatic tower at West Malling, variously claimed as a church tower or as a lookout or as a tower containing a lord's private room or solar, despite the lack of amenities such as a fireplace or latrine. Eynsford has a stone curtain wall thought to be of c1100-10 around an oval court like that at Rochester, except that there the material is flint rather than ragstone and the court is very much smaller.

Keep and inner ward at Dover

Probably of the early years of the 12th century is the rectangular keep of the royal castle at Canterbury. It contained two upper storeys of apartments over dark storerooms at ground level. The openings were round-headed in the usual Norman style and there are pilaster buttresses rising from a battered plinth set at intervals round the walls and also clasping the corners. The entrance into the central hall in the middle storey was reached by a flight of steps up within a forebuilding or porch on one side. At the end of the 1120s the archbishop of Canterbury began an even more impressive tower keep at Rochester, slightly smaller in ground plan, but higher, since it had four storeys, and still stands complete to the tops of the corner turrets. At Sutton Valence are remains of a much more modest tower keep probably dating from later in the 12th century. Of the middle years of the 12th century are the hall-block and upper part of the curtain wall at Eynsford and the curtain wall with square towers and a gatehouse at Saltwood. There are now only minor remains of the original inner wall of the bailey at Leeds and a bailey curtain wall with a rectangular gatehouse at Thurnham which may also have been built during this period. The bailey wall at Tonbridge is assumed to be of the late 12th century whilst the thinly walled shell keep which replaced the palisade on the motte may be still earlier.

Henry II, a prolific builder, is thought to have erected the vanished curtain wall at Canterbury. He is known to have begun erecting stone walls and towers at Dover in the 1160s. The scheme seems to have later been changed and the present inner bailey wall with fourteen rectangular flanking towers dates from the 1180s, as does the cubical three storey keep with four corner turrets standing inside this circuit of walls. The keep was the last and most massive of its type built in England, whilst the bailey is the earliest English example of a stone-built enceinte with all-round provision for flanking fire, earlier attempts at Ludlow and Richmond being more half-hearted with at least one blind spot left unflanked somewhere on the circuit. Pairs of towers flank the two gateways, the earliest example of this layout, previous gatehouses having been single rectangular towers, as at Saltwood. A considerable section of the outer wall at Dover, again with rectangular flanking towers, plus one polygonal corner tower, was also built during this campaign, although only part of this now remains.

In the 1170s, during a probable gap between the two campaigns at Dover, Henry erected an octagonal three storey tower keep at Chilham, one of a small number of experimental polygonal keeps of this period designed to overcome the problem that square keeps had blind corners which attackers could approach unharmed and which were vulnerable to undermining. This was precisely what happened to the keep at Rochester in 1215 during an attack by King John, and in a siege the following year at Dover a tower of the outer gatehouse was destroyed by mining. In both instances the defenders managed to continue to resist after the collapse. Indeed during the revolts against William Rufus in 1088, against King Stephen in 1139, and during the civil wars of 1215-16 and 1264-65, castles in Kent proved difficult to capture by force of arms. Several castles were destroyed by Henry II after the rebellion led by his sons in 1173-4. Whatever early stone buildings once stood at Allington and a long section of the curtain wall at Saltwood are thought to have been victims of this policy of slighting. Both castles seem to have been rebuilt in the 1180s or 90s, The thin curtain wall and one range of rooms at Allington being probably of that period.

After losing Normandy to Philip Augustus of France in 1204 King John continued work on the outer curtain wall at Dover. The wall is flanked by D-shaped towers with round fronts towards the field which had no blind corners and were supposedly less vulnerable to mining (although one was still destroyed in this way during the siege of 1216). The work of enclosing the outer enceinte at Dover continued during the first half of the long reign of Henry III. To replace the gatehouse destroyed in the siege a new gatehouse called Constable's Gate with a complex plan with several half-round towers rising from spurred bases was erected on the west side, whilst a second gatehouse, Fitzwilliam Gate, with twin solid round towers with beaks towards the field, was built on the east side. Henry III also rebuilt the damaged keep at Rochester with a round corner turret in place of the fallen square one and provided a round tower nearby at a corner of the curtain wall. Splendid new apartments were provided in this period at both Rochester and Dover but very little remains of them.

Constable's Gate at Dover

The erection of castles was strictly controlled by the Crown from the time of Henry II's accession in 1154 following the chaos of King Stephen's reign, when barons fortified sites as they pleased. From King John's reign onwards (1199-1216) the provision of embattled walls around a house required a royal licence to crenellate, only issued to those who were loyal servants or otherwise in favour at court. These licences help to date many late medieval buildings although it seems that in some instances nothing was actually built after a licence was issued, or not until a much later period. However we can be fairly sure that the several D-shaped towers at Allington and considerable parts of the domestic ranges there date from about the time of the licence issued in 1281. Also of probably of c1280 are the twin-round towered gatehouses at Leybourne and Tonbridge. The latter is a particularly fine building with round stair turrets facing the court and a splendid state room or hall on the topmost level. This gatehouse also functioned as a sort of keep, since it could be defended just as easily against an attack from the inner ward as from the outside, the passageway having a complex system of defences including inner and outer portcullises. It was built by Gilbert de Clare and is very similar to the east gatehouse of the inner ward of his celebrated Glamorganshire castle of Caerphilly. In the 1290s the Bishop of Durham erected a palace at Eltham with a wet moat around a thin outer wall with small octagonal corner towers. About the same time Edward I added an outer curtain wall with D-shaped towers and a new gatehouse at Leeds, whilst the old motte seems to have been encased to form a shell keep with a set of lean-to apartments around a central court. The artificial lake around this castle was probably formed somewhat earlier. It was held in by a series of causeways radiating from a barbican in front the outer gate. Also of this period is the solar block at Old Soar, not seriously fortified, but flanked by cross-loops in a latrine block at one corner.

Eltham Palace

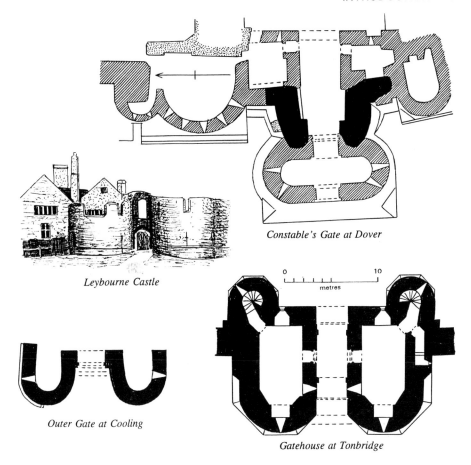

Constable's Gate at Dover

Leybourne Castle

Outer Gate at Cooling

Gatehouse at Tonbridge

Edward II issued licences for the crenellation of the mansions of Bromley in 1310 and Colbridge in 1314, whilst Edward III licensed Mereworth in 1332, Boughton in 1339, and Westenhanger in 1343, and Richard II licensed Cooling in 1381 and Hever in 1384. Not much remains of several of these mansions, but Cooling and Westenhanger have almost square moated inner wards with round corner towers. Both still have ruined outer walls but little survives of the domestic buildings, which at Westenhanger are known to have been quite palatial. Cooling has an outer court with U-shaped corner towers and both courts have twin-towered gatehouses. The towers of the outer gate have machicolated parapets, although the passageway itself was not so defended in the way that the gateway passages still are at Leeds, Hever and on the gatehouse with twin-round towers of the 1380s at Saltwood. Probably also of 1380s is Scotney, with an irregularly-shaped inner ward with four round towers and a square gatehouse and a rectangular outer court within an oval lake. Hever is quite a small moated courtyard house with the rectangular gatehouse as the only military feature and may be 15th century. The moated 14th century stronghouse at Ightham is about the same size. Other buildings which can be classed as stronghouses are Lympne and Nurstead, which both have 14th century halls adjoining plain towers of possibly earlier date. A third tower of this class remains at Stone.

Outer gate at Saltwood

A number of other manor houses in Kent were provided with moats in the 13th and 14th centuries. Some of them may be a response to periods of unrest during the reigns of Henry III and Edward II, but water filled ditches were not necessarily military in purpose. A moat was a permanent and efficient boundary for keeping vagrants, wild animals and malefactors out of manorial enclosures and would have been equally useful as a means of controlling the comings and goings of domestic animals, servants and members of the family. At all periods moats have been appreciated as scenic features and they served as a habitat for fish, eels, and water fowl which together formed a substantial part of the diet of the landed classes. A wet moat could also help to drain land otherwise unsuitable for agriculture or inhabitation. Moats were also used to flush away sewage so a house built within one would require a separate source of water for cooking, brewing and washing. Because of the many uses to which they could be put moats did not require royal consent of the kind required for the erection of embattled walls and towers. However they still had a function as status symbols since only those who held manors or a considerable share of one possessed the resources to create a moated house.

The words motte and moat clearly have a common origin and although modern historians normally understand them to mean quite different types of earthwork, this distinction was not so clearly understood in the medieval period. The spelling of the name of the moated house of Ightham Mote clearly illustrates this. Although excavations have failed to prove this convincingly, one might expect a gradual development from the conical mounds and ringworks of the 11th and 12th centuries to the low, roughly rectangular platforms which are the commonest type of moated site. The castles do tend to show this development from the oval shape of the inner ward at Saltwood with a fall away of the ground on one side to the almost square shape of the inner wards on flat sites at Cooling and Westenhanger.

Sutton Valence Castle

In the 1360s Edward III built a new coastal castle at Queenborough. Very little remains but old plans and drawings of it survive. It had a plan unique in England, with concentric inner and outer wards and an outer wet moat. The only features of the outer ward were a gatehouse with twin-D-shaped towers and a postern diagonally opposite. The inner ward contained apartments all around and must have been rather like the similarly-sized shell keep at Restormel in Cornwall except that the outer face of the wall was flanked by six large round towers, two of which flanked the inner gateway, which was set opposite the postern on the outer wall. Edward III also rebuilt part of the curtain wall at Rochester with two rectangular towers. The towers added by the Stafford family at Tonbridge also seem to have been rectangular. Probably also of this period is most of the curtain wall around the keep at Chilham.

At Canterbury and Rochester the old Roman city walls, which had been patched up in the 11th and 12th centuries when the castles were built against them, were remodelled during the 14th century with new gateways and flanking towers. At Rochester there was a considerable late 14th century southern extension, part of which remains with one tower. Another tower adjoins the older Roman wall. Much of the circuit still remains at Canterbury, with several round towers fitted with the new keyhole-shaped gunports developed in the 1380s for use by small cannon, and a very fine square gatehouse with twin round towers facing the field on the west side. Rochester once had a similar gateway on the east side. During the same period a palisade found on a captured French ship was used to enclose the town of Sandwich. Nothing now remains of a 13th or 14th century town wall at Dover.

Allington Castle

The Duke of Gloucester's mansion at Greenwich of the 1430s was licensed for crenellation but does not seem to have been fortified, but about the same time the Duke of Bedford surrounded the very fine mid 14th century hall and chambers at Penshurst with a modest outer wall with rectangular towers at the corners and in the middle of each side. There was probably a moat but no traces of it remain. The resulting building is perhaps classifiable as a stronghouse. The great mansion of the 1460s at Knowle has no defensive features, just an impressive gatehouse. In the 1470s Edward remodelled the apartments in the keep at Dover and rebuilt a couple of the towers of the outer ward, one of which has a gunport of that period. A single gunport also appears in the outer wall of the moated palace at Eltham, where Edward IV erected the very fine hall, still remaining fully roofed. By this time developments in cannon had made high walls and towers vulnerable. The moat and gunports at a place like Eltham simply enabled it to be held for a short while against a surprise raid or sudden uprising rather than to withstand a lengthy siege by a fully equipped army.

In the medieval period castle walls of rubble were sometimes lime-washed outside, making them look very different from the way they appear today. The keep at Dover was rendered outside up until the 20th century. Dressed stones around windows and doorways would be left uncovered. Domestic rooms would have had whitewashed walls decorated with murals of biblical, historical or heroic scenes mostly painted in red, yellow and black. Wall hangings decorated with the same themes or heraldry gradually became more common during the 14th century. Although used in churches, glass was expensive and uncommon in secular buildings before the 15th century, so windows were originally closed with wooden shutters. As a result rooms were dark when the weather was too cold or wet for the shutters to be opened for light and ventilation. In the later medieval period large openings in the outer walls sometimes had iron bars or grilles even if high above ground but they do not seem to have been used in the 12th century. Living rooms usually had fireplaces although some halls had central hearths with the smoke escaping through louvres in the roof. Latrines are commonly provided within the thickness of the walls and help to indicate which rooms were intended for living or sleeping in rather than just storage space.

Furnishings were sparse up until the 15th century although the embrasures of upper storey windows tend to have built-in stone seats from the 13th century onwards. Lords with several castles tended to circulate around them administering their manorial courts and consuming agricultural produce on the spot. Seats belonging to great lords could be left almost empty when they were not in residence. For much of their lives castles gradually crumbled away with only a skeleton staff in residence to administer the estates. Servants travelled with lords and sometimes also portable furnishings such as rugs, wall-hangings, cooking vessels and bedding, all kept in wooden chests. The lord and his immediate family plus honoured guests and the senior household officials would enjoy a fair degree of privacy, having their own rooms. Servants and retainers enjoyed less comfort and privacy, sharing of beds and communal sleeping in the main hall and warm places of work like the kitchen and stables being common.

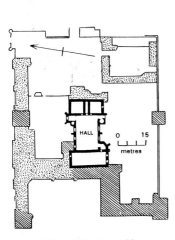

Plan of Penshurst Place

Deal Castle

After his breakaway from the Roman church Henry VIII became increasingly nervous of an invasion from France and took steps to defend his southern coastline. In 1539-40 a new harbour was built at Dover with a bulwark below the castle to defend it along with another fort further west, whilst three artillery forts, Sandown, Deal and Walmer, were built to defend the Downs anchorage, and another fort was built at Sandgate. At about the same time blockhouses or single towers mounting cannon were built at Gravesend, Milton and probably Deptford. These have vanished, and so has the Sandown fort, but the other three forts still remain. Sandown and Walmer had circular central keeps with four outer bastions creating a quatrefoil plan. Deal was a development on these with two six-foiled lower levels of bastions around the central keep. All of them had dry moats commanded by wide-mouthed gunports and the doorways between the various parts are carefully covered by pistol loops. Sandgate also has two tiers of outer bastions and a circular central keep but there the plan form is a triangle with curved sides and there is a D-shaped barbican in front of the entrance. Henry VIII also improved the accommodation at Dover and at Leeds, where he built an upper storey to the keep. During this period much work was also done to the domestic apartments at Allington, Hever, Ightham, Penshurst and Westenhanger. Elizabeth I kept Dover in good repair and in 1559 also began another fort at Upnor to guard the Medway estuary naval anchorage. It was remodelled c1600, the period of the present court on the landward side of the building.

Walmer Castle

Upnor Castle   *Upnor Castle*

By the early 17th century the castles of Canterbury, Rochester and Saltwood were in ruins and they took no part in the Civil War of the 1640s, but Sandown, Deal, Walmer, and Upnor all saw action. Sandgate was also garrisoned, and Dover was captured in 1642 when the weak garrison fell to a surprise night attack. New mansions replacing medieval apartments were begun before the Civil War at Chilham and Scotney, but the latter was never completed. Parliament had many castles dismantled during the 1640s to prevent them being reoccupied by Royalists. Most castles in Kent escaped this fate, being either ruinous or having been adapted to make them only suitable for purely domestic use. Others were required for further military use, but unfortunately in 1650 Queenborough was completely destroyed.

In the mid 18th century the medieval apartments in the inner ward at Dover were incorporated into new barracks. At the end of that century fear of invasion by Napoleon led to a drastic remodelling of the defences, new batteries replacing part of the medieval outer wall on the east and the rest cut down in height and strengthened internally by an earth rampart. Deal, Walmer, Upnor and Sandgate also remained in use throughout this period.

Deal Castle

Ightham Mote

Except for Dover, which remained in military use up to the end of World War II, the earliest castles in Kent are now ruinous. Dover is maintained by English Heritage, who also have custody of the ruins at Eynsford and West Malling and the later artillery forts of Deal, Upnor and Walmer, all of which have remained roofed and in use. Leeds has an early 19th century main block but the gatehouse range, keep, and the 16th century Maiden's Tower have also remained habitable. Allington is a private residence, having seen considerable rebuilding of the domestic buildings in the 1920s, and so is Saltwood where the earlier parts are ruinous but the gatehouse and several Victorian wings remain occupied. Of the later medieval stronghouses Hever and Ightham still look much as they did in the 16th century. Ightham is held by the National Trust, who also maintain Scotney, where just one tower and an adjoining wing remain habitable, and Sissinghurst, where the only medieval relics are two arms of the wet moat. Rather more survives of Westenhanger, where an 18th century house built against the outer wall forms a private residence, the walls and towers of this castle now being the closest that Kent can offer to compare with the superb late 14th century castle at Bodiam, just over the border into East Sussex. There are 20th century dwellings lying within the older moated enclosures at Cooling, Eltham, and Leybourne. The splendid late medieval hall at Eltham survives complete, despite being long used as a barn. Also still habitable are the stronghouses at Lympne and Nurstead, both with 19th and 20th century additions.

St John's Tower at Dover Castle

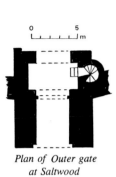

Plan of Outer gate
at Saltwood

Old print of Lympne Castle

Deal Castle

GAZETTEER OF CASTLES IN KENT

ALLINGTON CASTLE   TQ 752579

This castle may have been founded by William Warenne, created Earl of Surrey by William II. It was transferred to Lord Fitz-Hugh, whose heiress married a man subsequently known as Sir Giles de Allington. Massive foundations including a small west apse revealed within the court of the 13th century stone castle are thought to be a relic of stone structures erected by their son who was known as de Columbers, whose castle was destroyed in 1174-5 by Henry II. Until then the castle, which lies by the River Medway, comprised a small motte lying at the south end of an oval bailey with water-filled ditches and a thin curtain wall. The north arc of the moat was subsequently cut off by a new straight line of moat.

Allington later passed to Margaret de Burgh and in 1281 Edward I granted her and her husband Stephen de Penchester a licence to crenellate their house there. They added several D-shaped towers to an almost square court which was enclosed by a thin curtain wall in the NW corner of the original bailey in the 1180s or 90s. The rooms at the NW corner of the court are probably of that early date and the corner itself is buttressed and contains a latrine. Facing north beside this corner is the gatehouse, also late 12th century, although the small solid half-round turrets facing the field may be early 13th century. The entrance was closed by a drawbridge and portcullis and there are machicolations over the outer arch and remains of a barbican in front, these last two presumably late 13th century.

On the west side of the court are late 13th century lodgings of two storeys, the upper rooms being reached by external stairs on either side of a square turret facing the court. Loops on the lower level have original arches of yellow brick. A D-shaped tower backs onto these lodgings, and the larger Solomon's Tower lies at the SW corner. This tower is also D-shaped and has a spiral stair in a lobe on the south side. Nothing remains of apartments on the south side of the court. Serving them were the latrines in a rectangular projection and the fireplace set behind a D-shaped turret.

Allington Castle

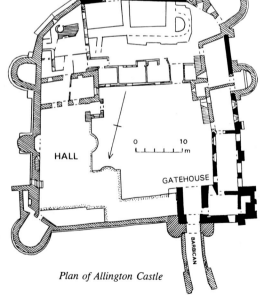

Plan of Allington Castle

Allington Castle

The east wall of the court was rebuilt in the 1280s and is slightly thicker than the rest. There is a D-shaped tower at the NE corner with a latrine projection adjoining to the south, and there is another tower near the south end of this side with a basement which is solid or had been closed off. A small D-shaped intermediate turret strengthens the wall behind the great hall fireplace. The only remains of this hall are the three service doorways leading to the buttery, pantry and kitchen, and a later medieval porch at the SW corner.

In the 14th century the heiress Joan de Penchester married Sir Henry de Cobham. Allington later passed to the Mowbrays. In c1475 Joan, heiress of Reginald Mowbray, married John Gainsford. He was attainted by Richard III in 1484 but pardoned by Henry VII 1485. In 1492 the decayed castle was sold to Sir Henry Wyatt, who set about repairing and improving it. The Wyatts added the twin-gabled range in the SE corner and divided the court by a series of offices with a timber long gallery above to link the chambers on the east and west sides of the court. Henry VII paid a visit in the 1490s and in 1527 Henry VIII came to Allington to meet Cardinal Wolsey, who was returning from an embassy to the French court. The king paid further visits in 1530, 1536 and 1544, but Thomas Wyatt was executed by Queen Mary for leading the revolt of 1554 against her marriage with Philip of Spain and the castle was forfeited. In 1568 Queen Elizabeth gave the castle to John Astley, Master of the Jewels, but he abandoned it in favour of the nearby palace at Maidstone. Some time during this period the hall, north range and NW tower were gutted by fire.

During the 17th century the surviving rooms were inhabited by the Best family as tenants. By the early 19th century the castle was owned by the Marsham family and occupied by two tenant farmers, but the west wing was abandoned c1840. Labourers occupied the SE apartments until in 1905 the castle was sold to Sir Martin Conway. By 1929 he had restored the building, rebuilt the long gallery, which had been destroyed by a fire in the 1820s, and provided new ranges on the north and east sides of the main court. The upper parts of the walls and towers were also repaired or rebuilt although one section of curtain wall still remains broken down on the south side. The castle was sold to the Carmelite Order in 1951 and is used as a convent and conference centre.

BAYFORD COURT   TQ 911639

The moated house of Bayford Court may lie on the site of a fortified house of Robert de Nottingham which later passed to the Cheney and Lovelace families.

BINBURY CASTLE   TQ 812602

Beside Manor Farm lies a ditched oval motte 40m by 30m on top. The house lies within a bailey 35m wide by 55m long with remains of a flint rubble curtain wall 0.6m thick on the north side with evidence of one square tower or gatehouse. This site is mentioned in a document of 1215-19, although it is not referred to as a castle.

BOUGHTON COURT   TR 034482

A rib-vaulted cellar below the 19th century Boughton Court may be a relic of the fortified house Sir Thomas de Aldon was licensed to build here by Edward III in 1339.

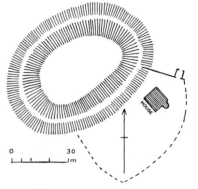

BRENCHLEY CASTLE   TQ 692428

This is a large, damaged ringwork with an outer bank set on a hill.

BROMLEY MOAT

The platform once known as Simpson's Moat has been built over. This may have been the site of a mansion for which a licence to crenellate was granted by Edward II in 1310.

Plan of Binbury Castle

Dane John mound at Canterbury

Keep at Canterbury

CANTERBURY CASTLE   TR 148572 and 146574   F

The Dane John mound within the SE corner of the city walls may go back to the time of William I, although there is controversy over its age and purpose its present appearance dates from the laying out of a pleasure garden here in 1790 by Alderman James Simmons. Domesday Book in 1086 records houses held in exchange for lands used for building the castle. In 1087 William II had some of the Saxon monks of St Augustine's Abbey imprisoned in the castle for refusing to accept a Norman abbot. A few years later either William II or his successor Henry I (1100-35) built a stone keep further west. Eventually a roughly rectangular bailey was created using the Roman city wall for its south and west sides and having a twin-towered gateway on the north and the old Roman Worth Gate on the south side. Compensation for land used to create this bailey was paid by Henry II in 1169. The Pipe Rolls record expenditure of just under £200 on repairs to the castle in 1172-4. The garrison of the castle in 1193-4 is recorded as one knight and 40 foot-sergeants.

In 1216 the castle was captured by Prince Louis of France. In 1221, during Henry III's minority, new cameras (private chambers) were erected beside the keep and the chapel, and repairs were carried out on the chapel and gatehouse. Hebrew inscriptions noted at the castle by Bridges in 1674 are thought to be a relic of when several Jews were incarcerated in the castle in 1277 prior to being sent abroad. During the rising of 1380 Arnold Sevaunce, keeper of the castle, was forced to burn the records kept within it. In 1390 £200 was set aside from fines for repairs to "la dongeon" i.e. the keep.

The Worth Gate was blocked up in 1548 and the city wall was then pierced by the new Wincheap Gate to the east beyond the castle bailey. Queen Mary had 42 heretics starved or burnt to death here in 1555-7. The castle was an abandoned ruin by 1609 when it was granted by James I to Sir Anthony Weldon of Swanscombe. A new sessions house was built on the site of the hall in 1730. By the 1790s the curtain wall had been destroyed except for the part formed from the city wall on the south side, and the ditch had been filled in. The top storey of the keep was demolished in 1817 and from 1826 onwards the lower part was used as a store with a gas-light and coke company. It was purchased by the city council in 1928.

City walls at Canterbury

The keep measures 26m by 21m over walls 2.7m thick above a battered plinth from which rise clasping corner buttresses, single mid-wall pilasters on the north and south sides, and two on the east. A forebuilding on the west contained the upper part of a flight of steps up to a doorway into a central hall orientated east-west. From the hall there was access through doors in now destroyed cross-walls to a private room with a latrine in the SE corner and a kitchen with a fireplace in the SW corner and access to a well and a service stair to the cellars below. North of the hall were a chamber with a fireplace and access to a stair leading both up and down, and also access via a mural passage to a small room in the NW corner. The upper windows were quite large and set in stepped embrasures. The basement loops are set high up and the embrasures are angled downwards towards the rooms. Sometime in the 13th century an extension with twin round turrets 4m in diameter was built or at least begun on the east side of the keep.

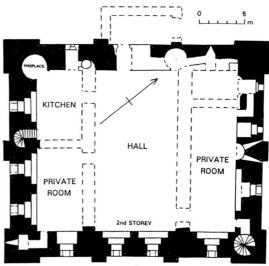

Interior of keep at Canterbury   *Plan of keep at Canterbury*

As originally erected by the Romans in c270-90 the city walls were backed by an earth rampart and enclosed 120 acres with four gateways. Parts of the Roman Quenin Gate still remain. The walls were rebuilt during the late 14th and early 15th centuries and provided with towers with key-hole shaped gunloops. On the SE the towers are D-shaped, whilst those reached from the cathedral precinct are square. On the west side the wall was protected by a narrow arm of the River Stour. The wall itself on this side was demolished by Colonel Ireton in 1648 after there were riots in the city when Cromwell and the Puritans proclaimed that Christmas was not to be celebrated as usual. However, one square tower survives some way south of the famous West Gate of 1375-81. This gateway survived the destruction of the other gates in 1648 and has a square main body from which project two round towers with keyhole-gunloops. Machicolations cover the space between the towers and the vaulted passageway has a portcullis groove. A room over the passage has a two-light window facing east and is reached by a spiral stair on the north side.

Gunloop in tower on city wall

West Gate, Canterbury city walls

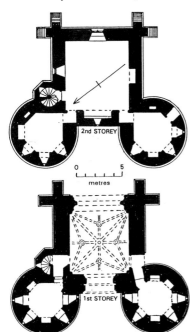

Plans of West Gate, Canterbury

West Gate, Canterbury city walls

Chilham Castle

CHILHAM CASTLE   TR 066534

Chilham was held by Bishop Odo of Bayeux in the late 11th century. He may have built the modest house of two storeys each with two rooms connected by a spiral stair in the north corner the lower parts of which were revealed by excavation in 1926. This was soon demolished, perhaps after Odo's rebellion of 1088, and replaced by a motte. Henry II spent over £400 on the castle in 1171-4 and the keep is assumed to date from that time. King John granted Chilham to his illegitimate son Richard. His daughter Isabel, who lived until 1292, married the Earl of Atholl, executed by Edward I for treason. Edward II gave the castle to Bartholomew de Badlesmere, whose eventual heiress after his son Giles died was his daughter Margery, who married Lord Roos of Hamlake. In 1461 Thomas, Lord Roos was attainted and executed by Edward IV at Newcastle. Chilham was then given to Sir John Scott, but he died in 1485 and Henry VII restored Chilham to Thomas Manners, Lord Roos, great grandson of Thomas. Lord Roos was subsequently made Earl of Rutland by Henry VIII, who purchased Chilham in 1539 and handed it over to Sir Thomas Cheney, Treasurer of the Royal Household. His son Henry Cheney sold Chilham to Sir Thomas Kempe. His granddaughter Mary married Sir Dudley Digges, Master of the Rolls. Their names and the date 1616 appear over the doorway of the fine new mansion to the NE. The Digges family lived here until they sold Chilham c1724. It was later held by the Skeffingtons, the present owner of the mansion being Viscount Massereene and Ferrard, although the keep, after being used for occasional banquets for some years, was sold off as a separate residence in the 1980s.

The embattled Digges mansion of brick with renewed sandstone dressings forms five sides of a hexagon open on the south and having the main show facade facing north with corner turrets and a central porch. This building presumably stands on the site of a medieval outer ward containing apartments demolished in the 1540s by Sir Thomas Cheney. Certainly there must have been a lot more of the medieval castle than survives now to merit Leland's praise of the castle not long before then as "not only commodious for use and beautiful for pleasure but strong also for defence and resistance". In 1861-3 a service wing was built between from this mansion out towards the keep. The keep lies within a roughly rectangular court or inner ward 27mm by 22m, the curtain wall being 1.5m thick and about 5m high. Although possibly of 12th century origin in its present form it is 14th century with some later repairs. At the north corner the wall is thickened externally forming a slim clasping projection, and there are other modest projections at the east and west corners, whilst the south corner is cambered off. Apart from the keep the court contains only a well house and modern toilets. It is too small to have contained much else.

The keep itself is a very remarkable structure, being an octagon 12m in diameter over walls 3m thick containing a basement and two upper storeys. The basement has three narrow loops, the hall above has two wide modern windows, and the top storey has a latrine on the SE and two windows, one being original. A turret 7.6m wide facing NE contains a wide spiral staircase onto which admits the existing 16th century entrance. This turret rather spoils the shape of the octagonal plan, but what destroys the shape completely is the thinly walled wing or forebuilding extending on the east side out to the curtain wall. This part has four levels, two of them corresponding to the keep top storey and the rooms are almost as big as those in the keep itself. This wing is certainly 12th century, although possibly very slightly later than the keep. It is built over the site of the 11th century hall block, one blocked arch of which remains visible below the end wall forming part of the curtain.

COLBRIDGE CASTLE   TQ 885479

The L-shaped farmhouse may incorporate modest remains of the castle which Edward II licensed Fulke de Peyforer to build here in 1314. The farm stands inside a rectangular platform and there is a triangular outer ditch. The castle later belonged to the Earl of Huntingdon and then passed to John of Gaunt, Duke of Lancaster. Sir Edward Wotton is said to have removed materials from the castle in Elizabeth's reign for the construction of the new mansion of Boughton Place to the NW.

COLDRED CASTLE   TR 276476

The tiny 11th century church lies within one of two baileys with a motte, with a noticeable rampart above the north and west sides of the churchyard.

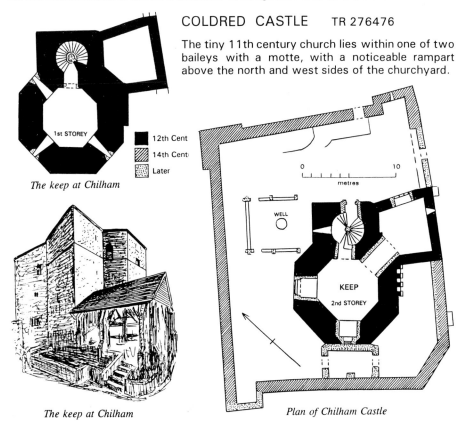

1st STOREY

■ 12th Cent
▨ 14th Cent
▧ Later

The keep at Chilham

The keep at Chilham

WELL

0   10
metres

KEEP
2nd STOREY

Plan of Chilham Castle

Outer Gate at Cooling before parapet was repaired

Inner ward at Cooling

COOLING CASTLE TQ 754870

A copper tablet on the outer gatehouse records "Knouwyth that beth and schul be, That I am mad in help of the cuntre, In knowing of whyche thyng, Thys is chartre and wytnessyng". A tablet as early as this is unique amongst English medieval castles. The castle was indeed built to defend the district, which was devastated by a French raid two years before Richard II granted Sir John de Cobham a licence for its construction in 1381, and the work was completed towards the end of 1385. The manor had been purchased by an earlier Sir John de Cobham in 1252. Some of the building records survive and show that the east side of the inner ward was built in 1382 at a cost of £456 with William Sharnal as master mason and Henry Yevele as architect. Thomas Crompe was the mason who worked on the outer gatehouse. In 1398 Sir John was banished to Guernsey but his estates were restored by Henry IV and he lived until 1408. His heir was a grand-daughter who married Sir John Oldcastle, who thus became Lord Cobham. He was a Marcher lord implicated in Owain Glyndwr's revolt in Wales and was a fugitive for several years before capture and execution in 1417. The castle then passed to Joan Braybrook who married Thomas Brook.

In 1554 Sir Thomas Wyatt defeated the Duke of Norfolk at Strood and then used the Duke's six cannon to batter the castle at Cooling for a day until the main drawbridge collapsed under fire and Lord Cobham surrendered. He was then obliged to join the rebellion against Queen Mary, and after it was defeated spent a period in the Tower of London. The last Lord Cobham was attainted by James I.

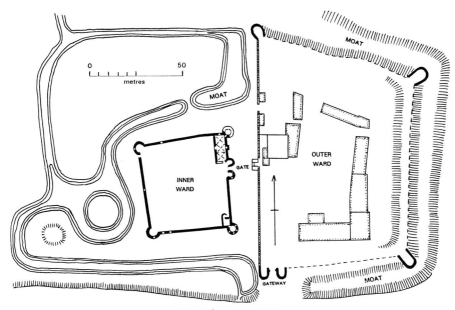

Plan of Cooling Castle

The castle consisted of an inner ward roughly 45m square originally protected by a considerable width of water on all sides except to the east where 15m away lay the 120m long west side of an outer ward 80m wide. The outer ward faced higher ground to the east and the 15m wide and 3m deep ditch there was probably always dry. There is no sign of a curtain wall around the outer ward, and it is possible it only ever had a palisade. Thinly walled U-shaped towers 7m wide project up to 9m at the NW, NE and SE corners and at the SW corner is the outer gatehouse on which the copper plaque is mounted. This gatehouse consists of a simple archway once closed by a drawbridge and flanked by D-shaped towers, the western one 5.9m wide over walls 1.5m thick and the eastern one slightly wider. The towers have loops with bottom roundels and are crowned with machicolated parapets rising 12m above ground. That on the eastern tower was repaired in the 1980s after part of it collapsed due to the failure of one of the corbels. The towers had no backs or floors or staircases and the wall-walk could only have been reached by ladders.

The walls of the inner ward are 1.5m thick and still mostly stand 7m high. At the western corners are 10m high towers 7.5m wide with open gorges. The eastern corners had towers 6m in diameter, of greater projection, and full rounds able to contain rooms. The SE tower stands 10m high but the outer part of the NE tower is now missing. In the SE corner of the court is a square vaulted room with a spiral stair adjoining. The NE corner has an undercroft 15m long rib-vaulted in three bays and extending as far as the northern of the two towers of the inner gatehouse which is 4.5m wide and 9m high and contains a spiral staircase. The undercroft is said to have had the solar above, in which case the hall must have adjoined it, extending against the north curtain wall. This side contains a postern and a drain and has a slight bend near the east end. The west and south sides also contain posterns and have corbels for the floors or roofs of other buildings set against them.

DEAL CASTLE   TR 377522   E

This castle was the central one of a series of three closely placed forts begun in 1539 to defend the anchorage of the Downs, protected to the east by the Goodwin Sands. By May of that year 1,400 men were busy on the three forts and the earthworks which linked them. It is likely that the designer of the forts was the Bohemian Steffan von Haschenperg, known to have been involved in the construction of the Sandgate and Camber castles on the south coast. He was dismissed in 1543 for lewd behaviour and overspending on various building projects. By 1540 the castle was occupied by a captain, deputy, porter and sixteen gunners so it was probably complete or nearly so. It is assumed that local men would help to strengthen the garrison in a time of crisis.

In 1648 the Parliamentary garrison at Deal followed the garrison at Sandown and the crews of the ships anchored in the Downs in declaring for King Charles. Despite being supported by attacks from Sandown and the fleet, the garrison surrendered after a three week siege by Colonel Rich. The castle was garrisoned throughout the Napoleonic Wars and in 1802 the governor's lodgings of the 1720s were rebuilt, only to be demolished after being wrecked by a German bomb in 1941. A monument in State care since 1904, the castle is now cared for by English Heritage.

The castle consists of a circular keep 86m in external diameter, flanked by six closely spaced bastions 11m in diameter, the whole being closely surrounded by a circular outer wall also flanked by six bastions 24m in diameter. The lowest level of gunports in the outer bastions look into a dry moat with a vertical outer wall. These openings are for handguns and are served by a passage backing onto earth below the main court and bastion interiors. There are ammunition lockers in the passage back wall. At this level the keep contains three segmental-shaped cellars and a central well from which a passage and steps lead up to the court. The north and south bastions of the keep are pierced by passages leading out to the passage with the gunports. A bridge over the moat leads into the outermost part of the west bastion. The south part of the bastion is closed off from the gate-hall to form a porter's lodge or guard room with a fireplace and a trap-door to a cellar or prison below. A gunport in the gate-hall back wall covers the outer entrance, the inner opening being set to one side.

Deal Castle

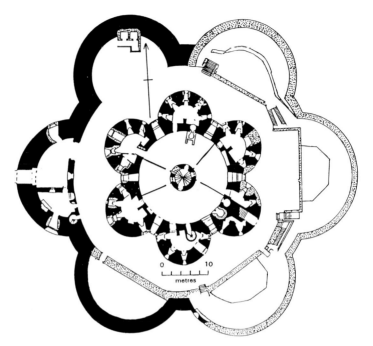

Plan of Deal Castle

The heavy guns forming the main armament were mounted in three tiers set upon the outer bastions, the inner bastions and finally the central keep. The existing parapets on the three outer bastions facing the sea are 18th century and are thinner and lower than the originals. The keep entrance faces SE. At this level the building contained barrack-rooms divided only by thin partitions. A stair in the south bastion leads down and a wider stair in the centre leads up. This is actually a double around the same newel, one serving the officers' quarters above and the other going straight up to the roof, where there is a small 18th century lantern. The ovens now in the common hall formerly belonged to the kitchen. The present layout of this floor includes a chapel but it is unlikely there was a chapel in the original layout. The bastions contained ports for handguns with roof vents to carry away firing-fumes. The fireplaces in them are all later insertions. A doorway later formed into the NW bastion has now been converted back into a gunport.

DEPTFORD CASTLE

The manor house of West Greenwich, existing in the 11th century, was known as Sayes Court when it was occupied by John Evelyn in the 17th century. The stone castle reported here may have been on the site of this now-vanished house or may have been a blockhouse defending Henry VIII's ship-building yard, the site of which is now occupied by an army supply depot. Queen Elizabeth's Lord High Admiral at the time of the Armada, Lord Howard of Effingham, also had a mansion here.

DOVER CASTLE   TR 326417   E

It is generally assumed that the great outer ditch up to 40m wide and up to 12m deep in places which surrounds the site is of Iron Age origin, although probably deepened and widened in the medieval period. The soil from it has been use to create a substantial outer bank. Dover was an important harbour as early as the Roman period and to help guide ships safely into it a pair of lighthouses were provided, one on the Castle Hill and the other on the Western Heights. A section of thick tufa-faced walling discovered by excavation in Market Lane and Queen Street may be have been part of a vanished Roman fort defending the harbour from Saxon invaders. In 1064, two years before he succeeded Edward the Confessor as King of England, and when held captive by Duke William of Normandy, Harold Godwinson recognised William's claim to the throne and promised to yield the fortress at Dover up to him. After his victory in 1066 William came straight to Dover and spent eight days strengthening the fortifications. Of defensive works of this period the only trace so far found is part of a rampart buried under the much more impressive 13th century rampart immediately south of the fine late Saxon church of St Mary de Castro. The closeness of the rampart to the church suggests emergency work by Duke William in 1066 rather than a slightly earlier work by Harold. The outer perimeter presumably had a stockade and must have then contained a small town with the royal castle acting as a citadel. It is possible that Duke William's castle comprised one bailey containing the church, another on the site of the preset inner ward, and a now-vanished motte or ringwork between them, as at Arundel and Windsor. Whatever form the castle took it seems to have remained a structure of earth and timber until the 1160s. It withstood two attacks by Kentish rebels in the period 1067-9 and when besieged by King Stephen's wife Matilda in 1139 it was only surrendered when the constable Walkelin Maminot decided to change sides and abandon the cause of the Empress Matilda..

The construction of stone defences was begun by Henry II in the late 1160s. Traces of a demolished tower of that date have been revealed SE of the present inner ward. However the main period of construction was the nine or ten years leading up to the king's death in 1189, during which £6,000 was spent upon building the walls, square flanking towers and two barbicans of the inner ward, the central keep, and a section of the outer wall on the east side, including the Avranches Tower, plus possibly the outer wall from there to the cliff-edge, now replaced by 18th and 19th century batteries, but known to have had a series of rectangular towers of 12th century type surviving at least up to the 17th century. The expenditure represents about two thirds of King Henry's annual income and is far greater than the amounts spent by him on any of the many other royal castles. In charge of the work was Maurice the "Engineer" who is assumed to have also designed the smaller keep built for Henry at Newcastle-upon-Tyne in the 1170s. The keep at Dover is first specifically mentioned in 1181 and was substantially complete by 1185, when it was stocked with provisions, but work upon it continued until 1188. Richard I (1189-99) spent whatever funds he was able to raise firstly on his crusade, then paying his ransom after being captured, and then on building Chateau Gaillard in Normandy, so work at Dover ground to a halt until after King John lost Normandy in 1204 and Dover became his first line of defence against the French. Between then and 1214 he spent over £1000 on continuing his father's outer curtain wall around the north and west sides of the site and on erecting domestic buildings, including a new hall, probably for the garrison, adjoining the outer curtain. The flanking towers of this period are D-shaped and at the north apex of the site was a gateway flanked by two of these towers. John is also assumed to have walled in the south side to fully enclose the inner ward, thus producing concentric lines of defence. Dover was thus the earliest of the very few fully concentric stone castles in Britain.

Constable's Gate at Dover

In 1216 the castle was valiantly defended by Hubert de Burgh against Prince Louis of France. The besiegers gathered on the high ground to the north and concentrated their efforts on the outer gatehouse facing them. Eventually they managed to undermine and bring down most of the eastern tower of the gatehouse. The garrison repulsed an attempt to storm the breach and used baulks of timber to block up the gap. They held out until after King John died and was succeeded by his young son Henry III, on behalf of whom a truce was made and the French withdrew.

Rebuilding and improving the damaged outer defences seems to have begun in 1221 and continued until 1256, the work costing £7,500. The outer wall was continued down the west side of the site to the cliff edge, the wrecked gatehouse was blocked up and reinforced, a series of tunnels and outworks were built to deny an attacker the ground opposite the north tip of the site, and a new gateway called Constable's Gate was erected on the less vulnerable western flank with a barbican outside on the other side of the great ditch. A secondary gateway, the Fitzwilliam gate, was also provided on the east side. Henry III liked his comforts and had a fine new suite of domestic apartments built within the north side of the inner ward. Finally the existing high rampart around St Mary Castro was thrown up with a new curtain wall upon it, presumably replacing an earlier curtain at a lower level.

Later medieval monarchs kept the defences in reasonable repair and adequately guarded. A set of provisions for the guarding of the castle survives from the time of the long late 13th century constableship of Stephen de Pencestre. During the hours of darkness twenty warders under the supervision of two chief warders were to keep a careful lookout in case of surprise attack and should the king arrive during the nigh he was to be admitted by means of the Fitzwilliam Gate. By this time a single person held the offices of constable of Dover and Warden of the Cinque Ports, the castle being his official residence. During this period the town was walled although remains of this are negligible. No 14th century work survives at Dover and only minimal maintenance was probably needed during that period. Humphrey, Duke of Gloucester, constable from 1415 to 1437 rebuilt the top of the Roman pharos or lighthouse to serve as a campanile for the adjacent church of St Mary de Castro. Edward IV (1461-83) is said to have spent over £10,000 on the castle, modernising the keep with large new windows, and rebuilding Fulbert of Dover's Tower and the Treasurer's Tower on the outer ward west side. He is also said to have rebuilt some of the towers of the SE side of the inner ward, although they have no features obviously of this period.

In 1534 Anne Boleyn's brother George, Lord Rochford, was created Constable of Dover and Warden of the Cinque Ports but in 1536 he was executed on a charge of incest with Anne just two days before her own execution. Henry VIII visited Dover eight times between 1532 and 1544 and much work was done in 1539-40, leading up to the arrival of his fourth bride Anne of Cleves. A new harbour was laid out for his naval vessels, guarded at the west end by the new Archcliffe fort below the Western Heights, and at the eastern end by Moat's Bulwark at the foot of the castle cliffs. These shore-level defences were needed because cannon of this period could not easily be fired downhill. The outer walls of the castle were repaired and the royal apartments improved. The Tudor Bulwark near the south end of the great ditch on the west side is probably also of this time. The first mention of guns in the castle itself is in 1548, when there were nine cannon mostly facing out to sea.

Queen Elizabeth stayed in the castle in 1573 but when she came again in 1582 she was accommodated in the town. About that time the northern towers and the church of St Mary de Castro were repaired and the pharos was converted into a powder magazine. Considerable work was done on the castle in 1624-5 when George Williers, Duke of Buckingham, was constable. At a cost of £2600 the apartments in the keep were modernised by Inigo Jones with new plaster ceilings and doorways ready for the arrival of Henrietta Maria, newly betrothed to Prince Charles. The French princess was used to great luxury and one of her entourage noted that "the queen was badly lodged in poorly furnished accommodation, and her companions were treated with scant ceremony, considering the occasion".

In 1642 the town declared for Parliament, yet the castle was held for King Charles. In August a daring merchant named Drake led a party of twelve men who scaled the cliff at night and overpowered the rather inadequate garrison of twenty men. The most serious of several Royalist attempts to take the castle was during the uprising of 1649 when the fleet anchored in the Downs went over to the Royalist cause. A siege battery was set up NE of the castle but the attackers retreated when Colonel Rich advanced on them before any damage could be caused by bombardment. At the Restoration of Charles II in 1660 it was proposed that Dover should have a garrison of 200 men, but in 1661 the garrison was reduced to just the Lord Warden and his household, one Gentleman Gunner and seventeen gunners, the latter probably concentrated at Moat's Bulwark below the main castle. From then until the Lord Warden transferred to Walmer, this official resided in Constable's Gate, whilst from 1689 until converted into barracks in the 1740s, the keep was used to accommodate prisoners of war, carvings by prisoners of this period still remaining inside it.

During the War of Austrian Succession in the 1740s the garrison at Dover was increased and what was left of the apartments in the inner ward were incorporated into new barrack blocks. The first landward-firing gun-batteries were erected in 1756. More drastic alterations were executed during the war with France from 1793 to 1814. The keep was provided with "bomb-proof" vaults at the summit, outer walls were lowered and reinforced with earth banks on the inside, the southern part of the east ditch was brick lined on both sides, and several new outer bastions and batteries were created, plus a network of underground passages and barracks. At the same time a huge new series of fortifications covered an area of the Western Heights three times the size of the castle, with a citadel (now a Borstal) at the west end, and the polygonal Drop Redoubt at the NE end, commanding the town. In 1861 a further outwork, Fort Burgoyne, was built on the hill to the north of the castle. These fortifications remained in use up to the end of World War II and one of the chief attractions now shown to visitors at the castle is the underground command centre dug into the cliffs near the SW corner of the site, complete with furnishings and equipment of the 1930s and 40s.

Colton Gate, Dover

Avranches Tower, Dover

Dover Castle measures 500m long from the Norfolk Towers at the north end of the outer ward to the cliff edge. The northern part of the outer ward is 180m wide, but further south the overall width increases to 260m. The area enclosed by the medieval defences is greater than that of any other British castle, and is even larger than some of Britain's medieval walled towns. Although much repaired and modernised internally over the years the central keep and surrounding inner ward still retain their late 12th century basic form, although the battlements are missing from the inner ward walls and towers. The outer ward walls have mostly been reduced in height for the requirements of 19th century artillery but are still essentially 13th century work with round flanking towers around the north and west sides, and late 12th century work on the NE. This section has two rectangular towers and ends with the polygonal Avranches Tower facing down an outer rampart at the point at which the line of defence is set back so that the wall running SW of the tower commands the outer ditch beyond. The causeway between the two ditches was probably the main entrance of the Iron Age fort but was severed by a ditch in the 19th century. The Avranches Tower has notable firing galleries with several loops served by a single wide embrasure internally, and the two rectangular towers further north have the same feature. Beyond these lies the Fitzwilliam Gate which was under construction in 1227. A postern with twin beaked towers, it led to a passage with a vaulted roof out to a gateway in the outer bank, thus allowing parties to sortie out across the great ditch without being seen. South of the Avranches tower lay the Armourer's Tower, from which a double walled passage led west to connect up with the east facing Arthur's Gate in the south barbican of the inner ward. Beyond the Armourer's Tower the medieval defences have been replaced by 19th century batteries, beyond which the outer rampart was flanked by three 19th century bastions (Horseshoe, Hudsons, and East Demi), with a fourth, East Arrow, placed still further out.

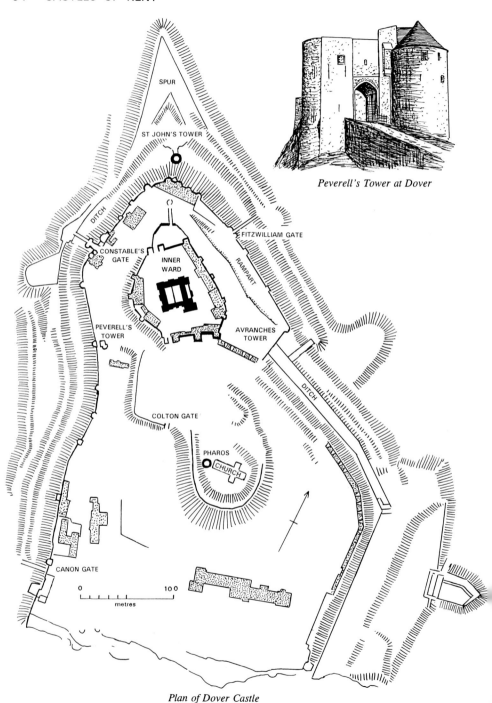

Peverell's Tower at Dover

SPUR

ST JOHN'S TOWER

DITCH

CONSTABLE'S GATE

FITZWILLIAM GATE

INNER WARD

RAMPART

PEVERELL'S TOWER

AVRANCHES TOWER

DITCH

COLTON GATE

PHAROS

CHURCH

CANON GATE

0   100

metres

Plan of Dover Castle

At the north end are the Norfolk Towers, a group of three towers formed by adding a solid beaked tower in front of the former gateway here wrecked during the siege of 1216. A passage from the north barbican of the inner ward leads down under these to the circular 13th century St John Tower standing in the middle of the ditch. This was a four storey building controlling (with a portcullis) a passage to an outwork beyond. These outer works were remodelled during the early 19th century when the redan was built on the bank with the spur beyond it to control this vulnerable flank, whilst the St John Tower (now stripped of its floors) contains a staircase linking passages and posterns. SW of the Norfolk Towers is Crevecoeur's Tower, near which are a latrine and a well. An early 13th century hall block backed onto the curtain between the rectangular Godsfoe Tower containing a chamber opening off this hall and the polygonal Treasurer's Tower rebuilt by Edward IV.

The next of King John's D-shaped towers forms the heart of the Constable's Gate built in the 1220s and still occupied by the deputy constable. Twin D-shaped towers rising up high from a spurred base down in the great ditch are set back to back to form a porch containing an entrance passage through to the older tower. The porch towers are liberally supplied with arrow-loops at several levels commanding the ditch. The approach was defended by a long narrow barbican on the outer edge of the great ditch, which was crossed by a bridge defended by two drawbridges with a postern cleverly incorporated underneath. The passage was closed by outer doors, a portcullis, and then inner doors, and was flanked internally by guard rooms added at the back of the original tower. Beyond the south guard room is a U-shaped tower rising from a spurred base, whilst beyond the northern one is a much larger D-shaped tower also with a spurred base, with a round latrine turret adjoining to the north. The result is an extremely impressive group. The north tower contained upper and lower guard rooms connected by a spiral stair and originally had no internal communication with the rest of the building. Over the passage lay the Constable's hall, with his vaulted private chamber set over the north guard room, whilst on the south was a lobby with a spiral stair and latrine. In 1882 extra rooms were added on the east side of the block and further rooms were created by dramatically arching over the re-entrant angles between the porch towers and those on either side of the main block.

Inner ward and keep at Dover

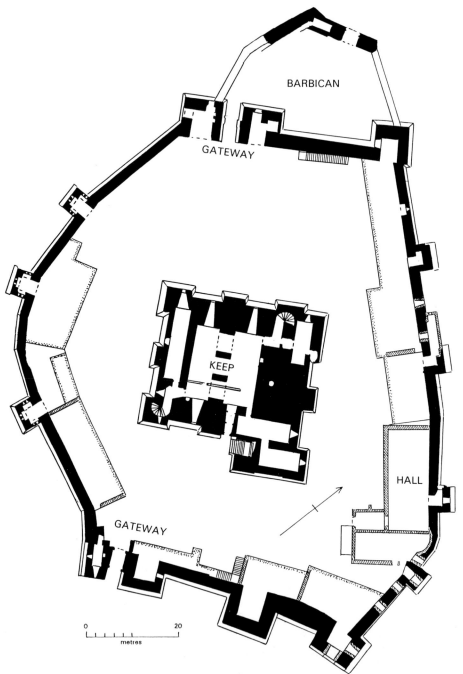

Plan of inner ward and keep at Dover

South from Constable's Tower the next tower is Queen Mary's, said to have been rebuilt by her in the 1550s although there is little evidence of that in the structure. Beyond here the outer bank is flanked by the 19th century Constable's Bastion. Peverell's Tower backs onto a gateway flanked by a south facing tower in a wall which originally ran east to the destroyed Harcourt's Tower. From there another wall ran east to the former south barbican and another ran south to swing round and connect up with the now-isolated Colton's Gate, a square tower, probably originally built by King John. SE of Colton's Gate is the late 10th or early 11th century church of St Mary de Castro. This is a cruciform building with a central tower the same width as the nave, but with the chancel and transepts somewhat narrower. The then ruined building was restored in the 1860s. Immediately to the west lies the Roman lighthouse or pharos, a square internally, but octagonal externally. It is 12m in diameter over walls 3m thick and is now 18m high, although the present summit is 15th century. Originally it may have been about 24m high. Enclosing the church and pharos is an earth rampart bearing foundations of a towerless wall of 1256. It ran round to the circular Clinton's Tower north of the church, then north to the Ashford Tower on the east outer wall. Set upon an outer bank beyond that around the church lay a windmill built by Edward I. South of Peverell's Gate the western outer wall has four D-shaped towers, plus the rectangular Fulbert of Dover's Tower, a 15th century rebuild with one north-facing keyhole shaped gunport. The Canons' Gate of the 1790s has replaced the Tudor Bulwark, and between here and the cliff edge the great ditch contains brick caponiers of that period, when an earth bank was built against the medieval curtain wall, filling the interiors of the lowered towers. Near Canons Gate is the huge cannon called Queen Elizabeth's Pocket Pistol. Reached by tunnels in the cliff is the much altered Moat's Bulwark of 1539, shown on an old plan as a timber revetted platform with a circular front to the sea. The semicircular battery now positioned here dates from c1750.

The pharos at Dover

The keep at Dover

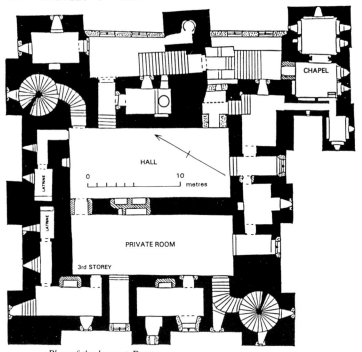

Plan of the keep at Dover

Chapel in the keep at Dover

The inner ward measures about 95m by 85m and has fourteen rectangular flanking towers with battered bases, most of them open-backed originally. Three on the curving west front and four on the NE are about 6m wide. Those at the almost right-angled north and east corners are roughly 8m square, as are the two which flank the King's Gate facing NW. The east tower of the Palace Gate facing SE is much wider than its western twin and the central tower of the SE front is the largest, about 10m wide. King's Gate is still protected by a D-shaped barbican, probably the earliest example now surviving in Britain. A still larger barbican with two flanking towers, a postern facing west and Arthur's Gate facing east, lay beyond the Palace Gate, but this area has been much disturbed by the erection of later barrack blocks. Arthur's Hall on the NE side of the inner ward still has one mid 13th century doorway but the apartments here were drastically altered by conversion into barracks in 1745-56. The king's chamber lay at the north end of this hall, whilst the kitchen and service rooms were at the south end. Other blocks on the SW and SE also contain some medieval masonry surviving the 18th century rebuilding.

Inner ward and keep at Dover

The keep is 29m high to the tops of the turrets which clasp the four corners and measures 30m by 29m above the plinth, excluding the forebuilding which extends along the NE side and round the east corner. The walls of Kentish ragstone with Caen stone dressings are over 5m thick but are honeycombed at all three levels with chambers, latrines, passages and staircases. They are, however, strengthened by mid-wall pilasters of a wider and deeper type than usual. The forebuilding takes the form of three towers controlling what were originally three open sets of steps rising to a doorway into the third storey. At the top of the second set of steps was a drawbridge. Behind the top of the third set of steps is access to a tank in which was stored rainwater from the roofs. Off the entrance passage into the keep proper is a doorway to a room containing a well descending over 120m to the water table below sea level. From here water was piped to various other chambers. The entrance opened into the largest of two lofty chambers forming a public hall with a private hall for the king beyond. The public hall has a latrine in the NW wall and, via a chamber in the east corner and a passage beyond, access to a fine chapel comprised of nave and chancel with rib-vaulting and blind arcading formed in the outermost tower of the forebuilding. A sacristy is formed in a turret flanking the outer entrance of the forebuilding and containing at that level a porter's lodge. From the private hall are reached two bed-chambers 7m long by 3m wide. Both have fireplaces and the most northerly has access to another latrine in the NW wall. Wide spiral stairs in the north and south corners descend to the lower levels and rise up to a gallery encircling the building high up providing an upper tier of windows (except for the NW side, which again contains latrines) and to the battlements. The existing top vaults are of c1800 and many of the windows and fireplaces are of the 1470s, but some have been renewed since and most are set in original 12th century round-headed embrasures. The storey below has a similar layout to that above with a larger public hall and a smaller private hall off which lead two bed-chambers. Another chamber is formed below the top of the forebuilding stairs with a small chamber leading off it, and there is a postern (15th century in its present form) leading onto the forebuilding stairs lower down, where the southern tower of the forebuilding contains a second chapel, a square chamber rib-vaulted in two bays. Two other chambers are formed in the SE wall below another pair above. The lowest level of the keep formed two dark storerooms lightened only by loops with steeply stepped cills at each end and connected by three arches in a thick cross-wall. Three mural chambers are squeezed in under the forebuilding steps (two of them have long been closed off to serve as cisterns) and there is another in the SW wall. These chambers actually have rather thin outer walls although there is nothing to indicate to an attacker that these might be vulnerable points. Opening out near the foot of the main stairs into the forebuilding is a postern doorway, a vulnerable point, although flanked by the forebuilding and closed with three sets of doors with drawbars.

Eltham Palace

ELTHAM PALACE   TQ 425740   E

Nothing is known of the nature of the manor house here belonging to the de Clare family in which Henry III stayed in 1270, and from which Edward I issued a number of charters. The estate was transferred to John de Vesci in 1278 and then in 1295 was conveyed to Anthony Bek, Bishop of Durham. Bek was wealthy and a great builder, and is said to have built here a new manor house surrounded by the still surviving moat, now only partly still water filled. Within the moat was a wall with octagonal corner towers about 5m in diameter with intermediate towers at least on the longest two sides on the south and west. Foundations of one corner tower still survive. In 1305 Bek presented the new house to the young Edward, Prince of Wales, but continued to use it, dying there in 1311. Eltham was subsequently a favourite residence of Edward, who succeeded his father as king in 1307. Edward's queen, Isabella, was often in residence, and here in 1316 she bore a son known as John of Eltham. Most of retaining wall of the moat erected at this time still remains. It has square or nearly square projections at three corners and a rather wider projection at the NW corner (in which is a later gunport), plus a series of brick projections on the west side thought to date from the time of Henry VII.

Window at Eltham Palace

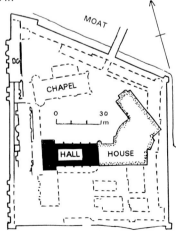

Plan of Eltham Palace

The great hall at Eltham Palace

Isabella's eldest son Edward III spent over £2000 on works at Eltham, which he much favoured as a residence after his mother died. A new drawbridge was provided in 1351 and then a new suite of royal apartments was erected on the east side, part of the moat wall being rebuilt to help support them. Eltham continued to be much used by the kings of England until the early part of Henry VIII's reign. Nothing remains from the time of Richard II, nor from the reign of Henry IV, who was married here by proxy to Joan of Navarre in 1402. Henry VI rebuilt the chapel and the Queen's Apartments but these have not survived. There is, however, still remaining a very fine hall completed in 1480 by Edward IV. Six bays long, measuring 30m by 11m, and 16m high to the apex of the hammerbeam roof, and of brick with a facing of Reigate stone on the north side, it lies almost in the middle of the moated platform and has a fine series of two-light windows (two per bay) set high up. The screens passage is at the east end with service rooms beyond and there are rectangular oriel windows projecting from the west end, where there is a dais. Beyond lay a long series of 15th century royal apartments in the west range. North of the hall lay a large court into which projected a chapel attached to the royal apartments. The chapel was of four double bays and had octagonal east corner turrets and larger stair turrets at the west end. South of the hall lay a complex of chambers and offices around several small courts. Little of these remain and our knowledge of them is mostly derived from a set of plans made in 1590 by John Thorpe, by which time Elizabeth I had allowed the palace to fall into decay.

After Charles I was executed in 1649, Parliament sold the ruinous palace to Colonel Nathaniel Rich. Most of it was then demolished for the value of the materials and the park was also despoiled. The site was subsequently leased by the Crown to the Shaw family, the first tenant, Sir John, repairing the moat walls and erecting farm buildings on the site of the older western royal apartments. The great hall was later used as a barn. In 1931 the site was leased to Stephen Courtauld, who restored the hall and erected a new house on the east side of the moated platform.

Beyond the north edge of the moat lay an outer court, probably of late 14th century origin, but the surviving part, the half-timbered west range with the Lord Chancellor's House at the south end, is early 16th century. Although Richard II is known to have built a new bridge over the moat the existing bridge of four unequal brick arches is probably late 15th century. Originally there was a drawbridge at the south end, where there is a fragment of the gatehouse.

Eynsford Castle

EYNSFORD CASTLE   TQ 547670   E F

At the time of Domesday Book in 1086 Eynsford was held by Ralph, son of Unspac, with the Archbishop Lanfranc as his overlord. The ditch around the site may go back to the 1080s but the curtain wall was probably built c1100 by Ralph's son William, the first of seven of this family who then adopted the surname de Eynsford. Probably in the 1140s or 50s William II heightened the curtain wall and built the hall block within it. William III was involved in the disputes between Henry II and Archbishop Thomas Becket, being excommunicated when he refused to allow the priest Thomas had appointed to enter Eynsford church. He is thought to have added the forebuilding to the hall and the kitchen in the NW corner of the courtyard.

The fifth William de Eynsford was one of the rebel knights captured by King John at the siege of Rochester Castle in 1215. The angry king was persuaded to ransom the knights rather than hang them. The sixth William, who succeeded him in 1231, was his grandson. After William VII died in 1261 Eynsford passed jointly to William Heringaud and Nicholas Kerriol, descendants of sisters of William V. The castle was seized by Ralph de Farningham for Henry III during the latter's war with his barons in 1264, and at that time it seems to have been out of use as a manorial residence, and the Heringaud share of the estate was then being enjoyed by the judge Ralph de Sandwich. This share later passed to another judge, William Inge. The castle seems to have seen another period of use c1300, probably by William Inge or a bailiff appointed by him. In 1312 Inge took legal action against Nicholas de Kerriol and others for having broken into his houses of Eynsford, Ightham and Stansted, and taken off his goods and livestock. Excavation evidence confirms that the castle of Eynsford was sacked at that time, and although the hall may have been repaired for use as a court house the place probably never served again as a residence.

Eynsford later passed to the Zouches and then passed to the Harts of Lullingstone, later the Hart-Dykes. A new house was built to the east in the 16th century and prior to a visit by the antiquarian Thorpe in 1783 kennels had been built against the inside of the castle curtain wall, although these had gone by 1835. Since 1948 the ruins have been in State guardianship, now English Heritage.

Eynsford Castle has a single egg-shaped court 54m by 38m enclosed by a curtain wall 9m high and 1.8m thick, outside of which is a ditch still occasionally flooded by the River Darent, which lies beyond the only missing section of curtain on the north side. On the inside can be traced the line of the original wall-walk about 6m up before the wall was heightened. Original features are the latrines at the SW corner, an opening which may have been the original entrance on the east (now with a much later well sunk in it) and a very shallow projection on the NE which supported a turret. Excavations have shown that originally the court contained a centrally placed timber watch tower, and the original domestic buildings are thought to have been located within an outer bailey to the east.

Lying detached within the eastern hall of the court is the lower storey of a hall block 22m long by 12m wide over walls about 1.5m thick. This block contained a hall with a solar to the NW over a pair of chambers used as offices or for storage. That under the hall has four loops in the SE end wall, one more loop facing SW, the well of a former spiral service stair and two square piers which carried the main beams of the upper floor. This room has no communication with the room under the solar, which has a latrine in the north corner and a well which once lay within the wooden watch tower. The hall was later given a forebuilding against the southern end of the SW wall with a long open flight of steps up to it. The block was remodelled after a fire in the mid 13th century and a kitchen was then built between it and the curtain wall. An older kitchen lay in the bailey NW corner, with a second well close to it. Only foundations remain of a tower added against the inside of the curtain as part of a new south facing gateway.

FARNINGHAM CASTLE   TQ 547670

Nothing now remains visible but excavations about thirty years ago revealed the footings of a 15m long section of curtain wall up to 4m thick and traces of a moat 12m wide and 3m deep.

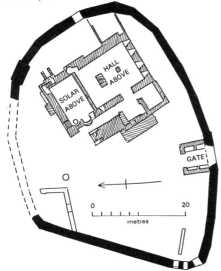

Plan of Eynsford Castle   *Eynsford Castle*

Eynsford Castle

FOLKESTONE CASTLE   TR 214379 & 230359

Remotely positioned high up on the Downs 135m above the port of Folkestone lies "Caesar's Camp", which despite its name must be Norman, but possibly an adapted older fortification. It is a ringwork 80m by 60m with a rampart rising 6m above the surrounding ditch. A U-shaped bailey 85m wide extends 110m to the east and also extends partly along the north side of the ringwork, whilst another bailey lies NW of the ringwork, which is thus defended by baileys on its weakest sides and has a steep natural drop on the west and south sides. Excavations in 1878 showed that the ditches were V-shaped in section and were cut in solid chalk without needing any revetment to the slopes. A well found in the ringwork had footholds spiralling down for at least 25m. Finds included a carved head of a man, a probable font bowl with arcading, and a penny from King Stephen's reign. In 1137 there is mention of the removal of the priory church to a new position outside the castle, although the site thus referred to could be the now built-up headland of Bayle above the harbour.

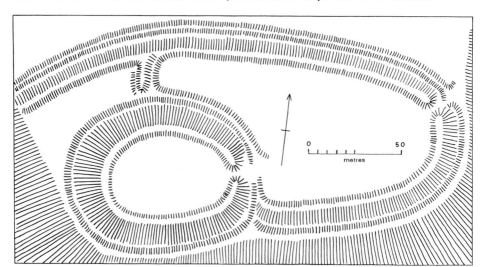

Plan of Caesar's Camp, Folkestone

GRAVESEND BLOCKHOUSE   TQ 654743

Nothing now remains of a D-shaped blockhouse built by Henry VIII in 1539, but excavations under the lawn of the Clarence Royal Hotel found traces of it.

GREENWICH PALACE   TQ 389773

In 1433 Humphrey, Duke of Gloucester, obtained from Henry VI a licence to crenellate his house of Bella Court begun in 1428 on land purchased five years earlier from the Carthusians of West Sheen. The mansion housed the Duke's famous library but does not appear to have had any defensive features. The house later passed to Henry VI's consort Margaret of Anjou. It was a favoured residence of Henry VII and his son the future Henry VIII was born within it. The latter also frequented the house, adding a banqueting hall and armoury. Here Henry married the first and fourth of his wives (Katherine of Aragon and Anne of Cleves). In 1516 Katherine of Aragon gave birth at Greenwich to the future Queen Mary, and in 1533 Anne Boleyn give birth there to the future Queen Elizabeth. Henry VIII also received a state visit from the Emperor Charles V at Greenwich and there signed Anne Boleyn's death warrant. By this time the house was a huge brick building with three irregularly planned courtyards and a tall gatehouse. The famous incident in which Sir Walter Raleigh placed his cloak on a muddy patch for Queen Elizabeth to walk on is said to have taken place on the Dover road just outside the south gate of the palace.

The palace itself has vanished but there still remains close to the site the Queen's House, begun in 1616 to a design by Inigo Jones for James I's consort Anne of Denmark. She died in 1619 and it was not completed until 1637, when it was occupied by Charles I's consort Henrietta Maria. She had extra wings added in 1662. Still further extended in 1807-16, the house is now the National Maritime Museum.

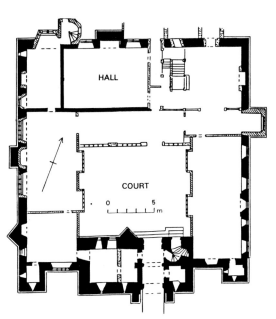

Plan of Hever Castle

Hever Castle

Hever Castle

HEVER CASTLE   TQ 478452   O

In the 1340s Edward III licensed William de Hever to embattle his manor house here. On his death the property was briefly divided between his two daughters, but the elder daughter, Joan, married to Sir Reginald de Cobham, purchased the other half. In 1384 Sir John de Cobham was given a licence to crenellate the house by Richard II and much of the building probably dates from that period. On his death Hever was sold to Sir Stephen Scrope, who died in 1408, leaving a teenage son whose wardship for some years was in the custody of Chief Justice Gascoigne and Sir John Fastolf (immortalised by Shakespeare as Falstaff). The castle was sold in 1423 to Sir Roger Fiennes. His brother and successor James, first Baron Saye and Sele was executed in the 1450s, and in 1462 the second Lord Saye sold Hever to Sir Geoffrey Bullen.

Sir Thomas Bullen served Henry VIII as an ambassador to France and the Low Countries. His younger daughter Mary became the king's mistress and Sir Thomas was made Treasurer of the Household in 1522, and a Knight of the Garter in 1523. He obtained a peerage as Viscount Rochford in 1525 and in 1529 was made Earl of Wiltshire and Earl of Ormonde. Sir Thomas's elder daughter Anne was born in 1501 at either Hever or Rochford Hall in Essex. She became King Henry's mistress and then in 1533, when already pregnant with the future Queen Elizabeth I, the king's second wife. It was she who first began to spell her family name as Boleyn. When Anne failed to produce a male heir the king tired of her and she was executed in 1536 on a charge of treason, having been convicted of adultery with four men, one of them being her own brother George, Lord Rochford, who was also beheaded.

After Sir Thomas Bullen died in 1538 Hever passed to the Crown and in 1540 was granted to Anne of Cleves, until recently the king's fourth wife, who had possession until her death in 1557. Hever was then granted by Queen Mary to Sir Edward Waldegrave, Chancellor of the Duchy of Lancaster. He fell out of favour with Queen Elizabeth and died a prisoner in the Tower of London in 1561. The Waldegraves held Hever until it passed to Sir William Humfreys, Lord Mayor of London in 1714. The estate passed to Sir Timothy Waldo in 1749. Prior to being purchased and restored by William Waldorf Astor in 1903 the castle had become no more than a neglected farmhouse. William made his fortune in America but settled in England in 1890 and was created a baron in 1916, and a Viscount two years before his death in 1919. Hever then went to his younger son John Jacob Astor, who was created Baron Astor of Hever in 1956. It remains with his descendants.

Hever is best regarded as a stronghouse, secure against burglary or a raid but not able to withstand a full siege. It is quite a modest building with a wet moat held back from a 1m thick curtain wall by a narrow berm. The wall encloses a space 22m by 24m, most of which is taken up by ranges of domestic buildings, leaving only a small open court behind the rectangular gatehouse on the south side. This front is quite impressive, with at each end tall but thin turrets containing tiny rooms with cross-loops with oillets, and the SE turret also has a keyhole-shaped gunloop high up. The roundels in the other turret are later. The only other original projections from the curtain wall are chimney breasts on the north and west, one of the latter being triangular. The gatehouse entrance passage is not centrally placed, having just a tiny porter's lodge east of it, with a spiral stair behind, whilst to the west of the passage are two levels of larger rooms. Above are two more storeys, raising the gatehouse considerably above the rest of the building, which has sections of battlements, but no continuous wall-walk. The drawbridge is flanked by stepped buttresses with blank panelling. At the summit the parapet is stepped forward on these buttresses with five machicolations commanding the entrance. The hall lies in the north range and now has a modern entrance hall in front of it.

Hever Castle

One or two 14th or 15th century windows with trefoil-headed lights survive at Hever, but many of the windows are the typical 16th century type of one or two or three arched lights under square hood-moulds, presumably insertions by Sir Thomas Bullen. The polygonal stair turret on the north also is of that period, but the windows adjoining it have a date 1584 over them, so the gables there must be Elizabethan, and the projecting bay on the east side certainly is. It was then a long gallery was created on the upper storey of the north range. The inner walls of the east and west ranges are early 16th century half-timbered work, almost entirely renewed in the restoration of 1903-7, the period also of nearly all the internal woodwork. However the moulded beams in Henry VIII's room are early 16th century work. The chimney piece with caryatids and an overmantel dated 1603 in the Morning Room in the NW corner came from Sparrow's House at Ipswich. A bridge over the moat links the castle with a series of offices and extra bedrooms built in 1903-7 in such a way as to look like a small village, and thus not overshadow the castle.

HORTON KIRBY   TQ 561687

Within a moat beside the River Darent is a Georgian house called Court Lodge in the south wall of which have been revealed two small square windows and an externally rebated doorway, probably 13th century.

Ightham Mote

IGHTHAM MOTE   TQ 585538   O

Ightham Mote is an extremely picturesque mansion 38m by 34m externally with a wet moat mostly about 8m wide except on the east, where it is narrower. The thinly-walled house has no defensive features but is classifiable as a stronghouse since it would be difficult to break into. There are bridges across the moat on the east and north but the principal access is though a gatehouse with four-centred arches on the west side, where there are many two-light windows with square heads. The east range is two rooms thick and contains a mid 14th century hall just touching by one corner with a vaulted cellar of the same period. The hall is spanned by an original stone arch and has an original doorway but the large window facing the court is of c1500. East of the hall there is a small open court into which projects a 17th century staircase and there is a tiny open light well north of the vaulted cellar. The south range has an overhanging timber framed upper storey and one 14th century window near the middle. Ightham was held from 1360 to 1374 by Sir Thomas Cawne but the oldest parts are probably a few years earlier. After Robert Cawne died in 1399 Ightham passed to his daughter Alice, who is assumed to have married one of the Haut family, since they held the house for the next century. Under Edward IV Richard Haut was Sheriff of Kent in 1478 and 1483 but was forfeited by Richard III. His son was restored by Henry VII and probably then built the gatehouse, but when a grandson came of age c1506 Ightham was sold to Sir Richard Clement, who in turn became Sheriff of Kent in 1531-2. The north range set over a loggia dates from about this period and the chapel over the vaulted cellar is certainly of this time, having a wagon roof bearing a Tudor rose with the pomegranate of Aragon, i.e. the period of Henry VIII's marriage to Catherine of Aragon. The house was later sold to Sir John Allen, and then in 1591 Charles Allan sold it to Sir William Selby, whose arms (together with those of his wife Dorothy) appear on a fireplace overmantel in an upper room on the north side, which also overhangs the lower walling with timber framing and has a later Venetian window. The Selbys remodelled the inner parts of the west and south ranges c1800 and sold the house in 1889 to Thomas Colyer-Fergusson. In the 1950s the house was sold to an American, Charles Henry, Robinson, who in 1985 died leaving the house bequeathed to the National Trust.

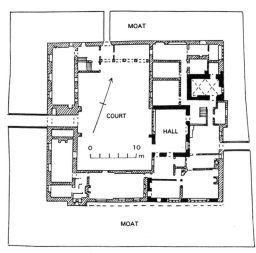

Plan of Ightham Mote

Ightham Mote

Leeds Castle

LEEDS CASTLE   TQ 836532   O

Haimo Crevecoeur obtained Leeds after the fall of Odo, Bishop of Bayeux, and in 1119 his son Robert founded the nearby Augustinian priory. At that time the castle is assumed to have been a motte and bailey structure, the present Gloriette no doubt being on the site of the motte. The castle was besieged and captured in 1139 by King Stephen. The family were dispossessed of their barony of Chatham by Henry III after the Barons' War of the 1260s and Leeds was granted to William Leybourne. By that time the bailey had stone walls with a gatehouse at the SW end and square towers on the NW and east sides. The artificial lake is first mentioned in 1272 but it was probably created a generation earlier. The barbican and mill must have formed part of the work of damming in the lake, and the mill certainly existed by 1298, when it was repaired by Edward I, to whom the impoverished Leybournes had sold the castle. Leeds was a favourite residence of Edward I and he built a new curtain wall outside the line of the old one, providing it with D-shaped flanking towers and a water gate. Lead for roofing the towers was purchased in 1298. If both circuits of walls ever stood complete at the same time the bailey defences would have been concentric, but it is uncertain whether this was case. The lower storey of the Gloriette or keep beyond the north end of the bailey is probably also the work of Edward I. He gave Leeds to Eleanor, his queen, and throughout the 14th and 15th centuries the castle remained part of the Queen's dower. Under Edward II Leeds was placed under the keeping of Lord Badlesmere. He joined the rebellion of Earl Thomas of Lancaster in 1321 and Lady Badlesmere refused to admit Queen Isabella, six of the queen's men being killed in trying to get in. The enraged Edward II besieged Leeds with a large army. After starving the garrison into surrender the king executed the castellan, Walter Culpeper, and sent Lady Badlesmere and her children to the Tower of London. Her husband was also later captured and executed at Canterbury.

Edward III also favoured Leeds as a residence and during the 1360s and 70s remodelled the royal apartments in the Gloriette, whilst it was Henry VIII who added the present upper storey rooms. The French historian Jean Froissart stayed here in 1395 when Richard was in residence, but the king was too busy with affairs of state to be given the book Froissart had brought with him. After his deposition Richard II was briefly imprisoned in the castle before being taken off to his ultimate fate at Pontefract. During a stay by Henry VI in 1431 his aunt Eleanor of Gloucester was tried before Archbishop Chichele and found guilty of "necromancy, witchcraft, heresy and treason", the sentence being life imprisonment in the castle. In 1552 Edward VI granted the castle to Sir Anthony St Leger as a reward for persuading the Irish chiefs to accept him as King of Ireland. However St Leger was accused of fraud shortly afterwards and died during the investigation. The castle later passed to the Smythe family and was sold in 1632 to Sir Thomas Culpeper. His son Cheney sold Leeds to his cousin John, Lord Culpeper, Master of the Rolls to Charles I. Catherine, heiress of Thomas, 2nd Lord Culpeper, Governor of Virginia (the family were granted a huge estate there by Charles II) married Thomas, 5th Lord Fairfax. After inheriting Leeds in 1821 Fienes Wykeham-Martin remodelled the Gloriette and built the Tudor-style block at the north end of the bailey, the two being connected by a two storey bridge replacing an original structure of wood.

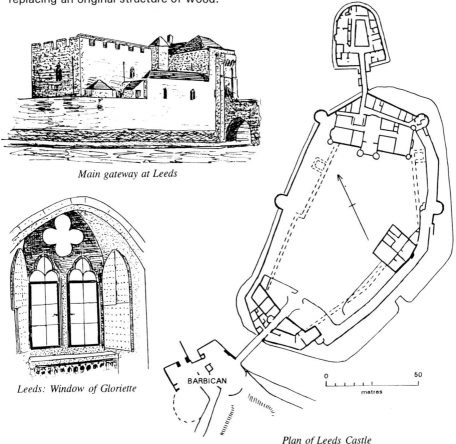

Main gateway at Leeds

Leeds: Window of Gloriette

BARBICAN

0   50
metres

Plan of Leeds Castle

Main gateway at Leeds

The pear-shaped bailey measures about 140m by 75m. The medieval outer retaining wall rising direct from the lake on the west side now forms no more than a parapet above the lawns, which lie about 4m above the moat, but originally the wall was rather higher. On the east side the lawn is curtained by a modern boundary wall roughly on the line of the pre-Edwardian outer wall, and the Edwardian wall is cut down to a still lower level and has a narrow lawn between it and the lake. The D-shaped towers are all about 8m in diameter. The NE tower has two storeys with timber walling on the straight side towards the court. It rises about 10m to the eaves of a pyramidal roof, but the other towers have been cut down along with the walls. The original 13th century rectangular gatehouse at the south end projected mostly within the courtyard. When the outer wall was built a new gatehouse was built between the two. Both parts had rooms on either side, resulting in a block that is two rooms deep. The entrance is recessed for a drawbridge and is surmounted by machicolations. East of it are blocked arrow-loops and Tudor windows. A stone bridge connects the gatehouse with a barbican in the form of a walled court 30m long from north to south with drawbridges connecting it to the mill to the west and to a pair of causeways on either side of a second lake to the south. What has been referred to as a bath by the lakeside on the SE side of the bailey was in fact a water gate with quite a wide passage lined in Reigate stone slabs and closed by a portcullis. Behind this feature is a modern swimming pool, north of which is the Maiden's Tower, a residential block built by Henry VIII but remodelled in the 1820s.

Leeds Castle

The Gloriette is a form of shell keep with walls about 1.5m thick above a tall battered plinth rising straight out of the lake to enclose the former motte. It encloses a D-shaped space 30m by 24m most of which is taken up by apartments on all sides, leaving just a small court in the middle. Most of the outer windows are of Henry VIII's time but some of the lower ones have renewed Y-tracery and must go back to Edward I's reign. The walls facing the court also have 13th century work on the south but the rest are an early 19th century stone replacement of the original timber-framed walls. There are latrine projections facing NW and NE. The largest rooms lie on the west, where there is a two storey projecting bay, but none of them are bigger than about 8m by 5m and there must have been a larger main hall elsewhere, perhaps where the 19th century block stands at the north end of the bailey. The interior fittings are ancient but mostly early 20th century imports from other buildings.

Leeds Castle

Leybourne Castle

LEYBOURNE CASTLE   TQ 689589

On the north side of a ringwork 38m in diameter SW of the church is a ruined gatehouse with two D-shaped towers, the western of which has a latrine in a round projection. Both towers have narrow loops at ground level and larger windows above. The entrance passage, once vaulted, was closed by a portcullis and has a slot in the outer face of the wall between the outer arch and the window above, allowing a fire lit by attackers in front of the gate to be quenched by pouring water down from behind the window sill. This a rare feature, but something similar can be seen in a gatehouse of c1271-75 at the de Clares' castle at Caerphilly in Glamorgan. Backing onto the east tower is a house built in 1930, beyond the south end of which survives a round turret. An engraving in Harris's History of Kent of 1719 shows the curtain walls as almost complete and enclosing a nearly rectangular area. The castle belonged to the Leybourne family and is said to have been begun c1260 but the gatehouse is probably of c1285-1300, whilst the earthworks could be older.

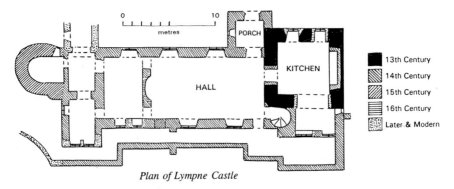

Plan of Lympne Castle

LYMPNE CASTLE   TR 119346   O

Lympne was the site of Lemanis, one of the Roman coastal defence forts, probably built in the 280s and abandoned about ninety years later when springs in the clay caused serious land slips. Fragments of walls over 4m thick survive with several U-shaped bastions.

Higher up, on the edge of an escarpment commanding Romney Marsh is the semi-fortified house of the archdeacons of Canterbury, held by them from the see since the time of Archbishop Lanfranc in the late 11th century. The 8.8m square tower at the east end with walls 1.4m thick is probably 13th century, although it has been claimed to be a Roman signal tower. The lowest level of this tower was given a fireplace in the east wall when it was adapted as the kitchen of a hall 12m long by 7m wide built to the west in the 1360s or 70s. This hall has a porch at the NE corner and a spiral stair at the SE corner and a pair of two-light windows on each side. The upper room of the east tower was then given a vault, a west fireplace, and windows facing east and north, whilst a doorway leads into a smaller room over the porch. West of the hall is a chamber of the same date and then beyond was a narrow cross-range once extending further south than it does now. Between the hall and the slope to the south is a rampart walk but there are no traces of any defences to landward, although it is assumed there was once a walled court with a gatehouse. Later additions are the U-shaped tower 5.7m wide with a spiral stair projection on the south which stands west of the cross-range, added by Archdeacon Chichele in the 15th century, the 20th century wing extending the cross-range northwards, and the 16th century fireplace in the hall west wall. The modern wing was designed by Sir Robert Lorimer for F.J.Tennant, who purchased the neglected building after it had become a farm subsequent to Archdeacon Croft having obtained the freehold in the 19th century.

Lympne Castle

MAIDSTONE CASTLE   TQ 760554

The palace of the archbishops of Canterbury close to the church and river does not appear to have been fortified. It contains work of various periods, mostly from the 14th century onwards although there is 13th century work in the so-called gatehouse and a ruined Norman building adjoins the churchyard. Leland c1540 mentions a castle at Maidstone in good repair. It could have stood where the house of Mote Park was erected in 1793-1801 for Lord Romney, unless Leland meant the archbishops' palace.

MEREWORTH HOUSE   TQ 669532

Edward III issued a licence for crenellating a house here in 1720. The present house on or near the original site is a Palladian style villa built in the 1720s to a design by Colin Campbell for John Fane, who inherited the earldom of Westmorland in 1736.

MILTON BLOCKHOUSE & MOAT   TQ 918660

Nothing now remains of a D-shaped blockhouse known as Cobham's Bulwark built to guard the Swale in 1539 by Henry VIII. The grid reference given is that of a moated platform probably of 13th or 14th century date known as Castle Rough on the west bank of Milton Creek. The blockhouse probably lay NE of this.

NEWENDEN CASTLE   TQ 852284

The outer bailey of this low lying motte and bailey site amongst marshland is thought to be a relic of a Saxon burgh. The earthworks have suffered from settlement.

NEWNHAM CASTLE   TQ 955579

The earthworks of this motte and bailey site were much damaged in 1957 and only slight traces of the bailey now remain.

NURSTEAD COURT   TQ 641685

Nurstead Court consists of half of a 14th century aisled hall with a huge hipped roof, a Tudor-style east range of c1840, and adjoining the hall NW corner a ruined rectangular building with thick walls of banded flint and stone, perhaps a 14th century tower house, although its actual date and purpose remain uncertain.

Latrine block at Old Soar

OLD SOAR   TQ 619541   O

Of the chief seat of the Culpeper family there remains a solar of c1290 raised over a vaulted basement which lay at the east end of a timber hall 10m wide. At the NE corner the solar block has a thinly-walled latrine wing with cross-shaped arrow-loops in all four walls. At the SE corner is a wing with a chapel over a basement.

Plan of Old Soar

Penshurst Place

PENSHURST PLACE   TQ 527439   O

The very fine hall block in the centre of the site was built by the rich London merchant, Sir John Pulteney, four times Lord Mayor of the city in the 1330s. The hall measures about 18m by 11m and is of four bays with a central heath. There is a dais at the west end and a screens passage at the east end onto which open north and south doorways with two storey porches and three service doorways, two of them to a buttery and pantry and the central one to a passage to a former octagonal kitchen further east which was destroyed c1836. There is a single upper chamber over the buttery and pantry and there were family apartments to the west. The hall has lofty two-light windows with transoms. The whole building is embattled, as allowed by a licence to crenellate granted by Edward III in 1341, but it was not in any way defensible and as far as is known it was originally without any outer defences.

In 1393 Richard II granted Sir John Devereux a licence to fortify Penshurst but he died the following year and it appears that the outer walls and towers eventually built were the work of John of Lancaster, Duke of Bedford, uncle and regent for the young Henry VI, Duke John having purchased the site in 1430. Of the walls themselves, which enclosed a space about 90m east west by 70m wide, there remain only a short section on the west, adjoining a block known as the Buckingham Building containing a hall even larger than the older one, plus stumps of walls on each side of a square gatehouse called the Kitchen Tower in the middle of the south side. Originally there were eight towers in all, four at the corners, and four intermediate ones. Parts of the northern gatehouse (the King's Tower) and the NW and SW towers survive incorporated into the complex of rooms around the west and north sides of the site.

Edward VI granted Penshurst to Sir Henry Sidney in 1552. He remodelled the family rooms, provided the screen in the 14th century hall, and then incorporated the north gatehouse into a north range with an open arcade (now glazed) with Tuscan columns facing south. This work is dated 1579 on a rainwater-head and was probably the earliest building in England to feature an open loggia. Also of this period is the SW wing dated 1574 and 1575 containing a long gallery which was panelled c1620. Among the portraits in the gallery are those of Edward VI, Elizabeth I, Sir Henry, his daughter Mary and his famous son, Sir Philip. Sir Henry, who died in 1587, also added a tall octagonal turret to the older SW tower. Penshurst survived the 17th and 18th centuries with very little alteration. The west front bears the date 1818, when it was mostly rebuilt from a very decayed state for Sir John Shelley Sidney, who inherited the house that year. The north front was also then mostly refaced.

Penshurst Place

QUEENBOROUGH CASTLE   TQ 912722

In 1361-77 Edward erected a new castle here to guard against French raids, although he also stayed within it frequently, so it was not purely military in purpose. The castle was accompanied by a new town given a charter in 1368 and which had two MPs until the reforms of 1832, the cost of building the two together being over £25,000. The name Queenborough is a reminder that custody was given to Edward's consort Philippa of Hainault. During Cade's rebellion of 1450 the castle was held against the rebels by Sir Roger Chamberllyn with a garrison of 22 men. The castle was strengthened by Henry VIII in the 1530s and it was repaired by Queen Elizabeth. At the time of the Armada in 1588 the constable was Sir Edward Hoby, who had custody of the Spaniard Signor Jeromino, captured by Francis Drake.

The town never prospered and only humps and bumps now remain of the castle, 0.5km inland from the church, as a result of it being destroyed on Cromwell's orders in 1650. Luckily plans and drawings of the castle have survived and although the engraving shown below suffers from vertical distortion (it is unlikely that the towers were much taller than just over twice their diameter) we have a fair idea of what it looked like. Designed by the king's mason John Box, it had a plan unique in Britain with a circular inner ward about 30m in diameter within a 3m thick wall flanked by six round towers about 10m in diameter, two of which were placed closer together to flank the inner gateway. The inner ward had a well (which was wrecked by an earthquake in 1382) lying in the centre of an open court 16m across with chambers between it and the outer wall. These rooms were divided by double-walled corridors from the court into the tower basements. Surrounding the inner ward to produce a concentric plan was a circular outer ward 90m in diameter within a wall about 3m thick outside of which was a moat 10m wide. This outer curtain wall was pierced by a postern gate opposite the inner gate, but the main entrance, with two round towers, the only projections from the outer ward wall, lay opposite, so that it was necessary to circumnavigate half of the inner ward to get from the main outer gate to the inner gate. Parallel walls built between the inner and outer curtain walls within each of the outer gate and postern allowed the control of movements of intruders.

Old print of Queenborough Castle

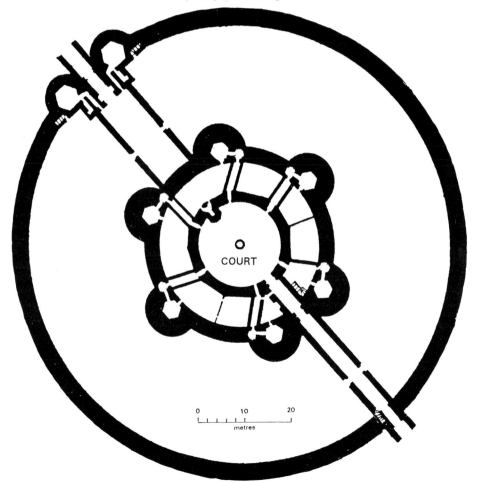

COURT

0   10   20
metres

Plan of Queenborough Castle

ROCHESTER CASTLE   TQ 741686   E

King William I is mentioned as having a castle here in the Domesday Book of 1086, the bishop having been compensated for the land taken for it. This castle was an earth and timber building on the site now known as Boley Hill lying outside the SW corner of the Roman city walls. Until his disgrace and imprisonment in 1082 it was held, along with the earldom of Kent, by the king's half brother, Odo, Bishop of Bayeux. In 1088 the castle became the headquarters of a rebellion led by Bishop Odo, his brother Robert, Count of Mortain and several other notable lords. Odo and Robert were captured by William II after he besieged them at Pevensey Castle in Sussex. Odo was sent to Rochester to tell the garrison to submit to the king. The rebels sortied out from the city walls and carried Odo back to the fortifications. The king then besieged Rochester but was unable to take it by force of arms. The garrison eventually surrendered on terms allowing them to leave with their horses and arms, although they lost their English lands. It was probably immediately after this siege that a new castle with a stone curtain wall was built for the king under the supervision of Bishop Gundulph to the north of the old site and just 170m west of the cathedral. Gundulph is stated to have been "very competant and skilful at building in stone". The tower on the north side of the cathedral is said to be his work and he is known to have been involved in the construction of the White Tower at London.

Henry I granted custody of Rochester Castle to William de Corbeil, Archbishop of Canterbury together with permission to build the existing tower keep. The many knights owing castle guard duty at the castle were to continue to give service there. During periods when the archbishopric was vacant there are records of royal expenditure on the castle, over £100 being spent on it by Henry II during the rebellion of 1172-3, whilst King John spent £115 on repairs to the keep, bridge, buildings and clearing out the moat in 1206. John fell out with Archbishop Stephen Langton and made an agreement with him for the castle to be held by Reginald de Cornhill.

Interior of keep at Rochester

In 1215 Reginald de Cornhill handed over the castle (which he was then holding for the archbishop) to the rebel barons. Archbishop Langton was denounced as a traitor and his successors lost custody of the castle, which was soon being besieged by the king after he entered the city in a surprise attack in mid October. A contemporary chronicler commented that "our age has not known a siege so hard pressed or so strongly resisted" and said afterwards "few cared to put their trust in castles". The defences were battered by catapults and either these or mining eventually breached the bailey wall. In late November the king commanded his justiciar, Hubert de Burgh, to "send us with all speed by day and night forty of the fattest pigs of the sort least good for eating to bring fire beneath the tower". These were required to burn the wooden props in a mine underneath the keep south corner. Even after this corner was thus destroyed the rebels continued to resist for a day or two, having retreated behind the cross-wall. However they soon ran out of provisions, and, having expelled some of their number, who suffered mutilation by the attackers, they finally submitted. The king wanted to hang all the rebels but in the event only one crossbowman was so treated, most of the others, including Reginald de Cornhill and William de Albini, being incarcerated at Corfe Castle in Dorset.

The much-damaged castle is assumed to have been easily captured in 1216 by Prince Louis of France, but no record of such an event survives. By 1217 it was back in royal hands and £680 was spent on repairs over the next twenty years, most of it on rebuilding the corner of the keep and erecting a corner tower on the bailey wall nearby, whilst another £300 was spent on a new ditch along the south side of the city to also enclose the old Boley Hill site which had been used by the attackers in 1215. There is mention of the building of a new chapel and chamber in 1221. A new drawbridge and brattice were provided for the now-vanished SW gate facing Boley Hill in 1224-5, and this gate and the main gate facing the city were repaired in 1237. Not until 1232 was the keep finally provided with new floors and a roof. In 1239 Henry III ordered the castle chapel to be plastered and provided with a wall-painting of Christ in Majesty. A new timber-framed chapel of St Margaret was erected beside the royal apartments at a cost of £132. Both chapels were wainscoted in 1247 and the hall windows were given stained glass with figures of the king and armorial bearings. New stables and an almonry were erected in 1248, and in 1249-50 £150 was spent on rebuilding the main gateway towards the city. St Margaret's chapel was provided with direct access from the outside rather than just through the king's chamber in 1254, the keep was repaired in 1256, and there were further repairs to the keep and main gate in 1258-9.

In April 1264 Gilbert de Clare, Earl of Gloucester advanced from Tonbridge to Rochester, which was held against the rebel barons for Henry III by Roger de Leybourne. Simon de Montfort, Earl of Leicester, approached from London and managed to cross the Medway by means of using a fireship as a smoke screen. The two earls stormed the city, and on the next day the castle bailey was captured. It appears that the attackers then attempted to undermine the keep as in 1215 but after a week the two earls were forced to retire when Henry III and Prince Edward advanced against them. The castle was left in a much damaged state, the defenders having themselves burnt down the hall when the siege began, and it appears that parts of the castle were left ruinous for over a century. In 1275 it was reported that materials from the buildings had been stolen for use elsewhere, and in 1281 the constable, John de Cobham was allowed to demolish the gutted chambers and use the stone elsewhere within the castle. A survey of 1340 estimates the cost of adequate repairs at £600, whilst in 1363 another survey then stated the repairs would cost over £3300.

Keep at Rochester

Between 1367 and 1370 Edward III finally had the castle refurbished at a cost of £2262. The keep, hall, chambers and gateways were all repaired and two rectangular towers built on the east side. A new drawbridge for the main gate is mentioned in 1370. Further work was executed just before the king's death in 1377, and his grandson Richard II also spent £500 on the fabric, some of it perhaps repairs after the Peasants Revolt of 1381, whilst a new bastion overlooking the bridge over the Medway was erected at the NW corner of the bailey.

The castle rapidly decayed during the 15th and 16th centuries and there are no records of the crown spending anything on repairs. James I granted the ruins to Sir Anthony Weldon and they remained in the hands of his descendants until purchased by the Corporation of Rochester for use as a pleasure garden in 1884, a lease for the same purpose having been in force since 1870. The site was transferred into state care in 1965, and is now maintained by English Heritage.

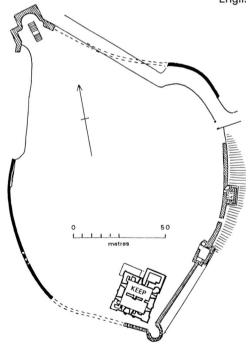

Plan of Rochester Castle

Tower at Rochester

West curtain wall at Rochester

About two thirds of the circuit of the curtain wall of the castle of the 1080s survives, enough to show its general shape and size of about 130m by 110m. The section of wall facing the river is original work, but set on the foundations of the Roman city wall, repaired in the 13th century and underpinned in the 1870s. The battlements still remain on the central section of this wall. The fragment on the north is also original, but the eastern walls are a 14th century rebuilding with four construction arches now visible, but once buried in an earth bank. All around this side was a wide outer ditch. This large enclosure was subsequently divided by a cross-wall into an inner bailey containing the keep at the south end and a larger outer bailey to the north. No trace remains of the cross-wall or of its gatehouse, which is mentioned in several medieval documents, nor are there any traces of the main outer gatehouse at the NE corner, facing the city, or the south gate close to the keep. These features had all vanished by the time of a map of Rochester made in 1717. The evidence of a Buck brothers print of 1735 suggests that Edward III added a barbican with twin turrets in front of a square 11th century gatehouse and a stone bridge was later built out across the moat. The only traces of Henry III's domestic buildings are four round-arched embrasures pierced through the west wall, plus traces further north against the curtain of a vaulted undercroft, above which are the blocked embrasures of a pair of two-light windows for a hall or other important chamber.

When the NW bastion was added by Richard II new walls were built out to meet it, slightly extending the area of the outer bailey at this corner. This bastion still remains in a much altered and ruined state, with a entrance of c1872 broken through it. A second Buck print of 1735 shows a wall linking this bastion to the bridge over the Medway, which then came right up to the bastion, in which was a shaft for hoisting up supplies from boats. At the south corner, close to the keep, is a U-shaped tower or bastion 9m across built in the 1220s and containing two levels of firing loops. The curtain west of this bastion must be of similar date, having further firing loops in it. Between the bastion and the site of the NE gateway are two rectangular towers of the 1360s. The still-habitable northern tower contains a vault. It projects entirely outside the curtain and has a spiral stair in a projection at the NW corner and a latrine in the SW corner. The southern tower straddles the curtain and is said to replace an 11th or 12th century tower on this site. Both towers are of two storeys and have broad battered bases towards the field.

Tower on city wall, Rochester

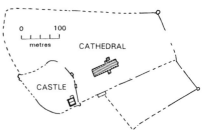

Plan of the city at Rochester

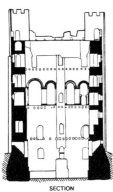

SECTION

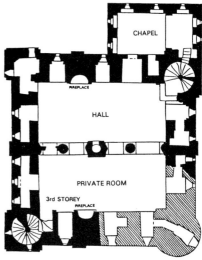

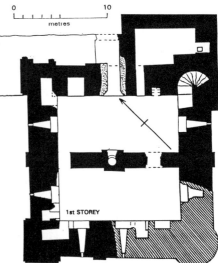

Plans of the keep at Rochester

Although it lacks a roof or any floors, Archbishop Corbeil's tower keep of c1128-35 is one of the best preserved and most impressive examples of its type in Britain. It measures 21m by 22m above a battered plinth mostly buried below ground. Rising from this plinth are the turrets clasping the corners and a single pilaster buttress near the middle of each side. Externally the keep is 27m high to the top of the crumbled merlons, and an extra 5m to the top of the four corner turrets, whilst internally it is still higher, the floor of the lowest of the four lofty storeys being 3m below ground. The whole southern quarter of the building was rebuilt in the 1220s after being destroyed by mining in 1215 and the turret there was then made round instead of square. Chevrons and nook-shafts appear on the uppermost embrasures of the original parts, but these were not repeated in the rebuilt part. A set of steps runs round the north corner, through the remains of a tower and up over a drawbridge pit to a forebuilding containing an ante-room with three two-light windows facing NE. From here a doorway once closed by a portcullis and a door leads into the second storey of the main tower. It does not appear that portcullises were a common feature of Norman keeps and this is the earliest securely dated example of a portcullis being used in any fortification in Britain.

The chamber into which the doorway leads is a hall probably for the use of the constable and having a fireplace, access to the well in the cross-wall which divides all the levels of the keep, a postern doorway set high up in the keep SE wall and chamber in the north corner, from which was reached a room in the tower commanding the main steps. In the east corner is a wide spiral staircase linking all the levels of the keep. Another stair in the west corner only serves the rooms from this level upwards. The basement rooms have only tiny slits for light and must have been very dark. Below the drawbridge pit in front of the forebuilding, which contains a prison at this level with a cesspit below, a entrance has been broken through the 3.3m thick main wall in modern times. The third storey contains the main state chambers, and the cross-wall here is pierced by pairs of arches on either side of the central well. This pattern is repeated at the level of a gallery with a wall passage round all four sides of the keep linking an upper set of windows for this storey. The upper windows are now mostly just ragged holes externally but originally some were of two lights. One of these, opening off the gallery, survives intact, having been blocked when the roof of the chapel in the forebuilding was later altered and then opened out again in the 1890s. This chapel was entered through an embrasure serving as the portcullis chamber (a very inconvenient arrangement) and was divided into a nave and chancel. In later times an opening was broken through from the chancel sedilia recess to the eastern staircase. The two rooms on the topmost storey formed a hall and chamber for the private use of the archbishop. Each room has triple sets of window embrasures linked by galleries facing NW and the eastern room also has linked window embrasures on the other sides.

A few fragments still remain of the stone wall built in the early 3rd century in front of the earlier earth rampart of the Roman town of Durobrivae. The 14th century East Gate at the end of the High Street has gone but it seems to have been similar to the West Gate at Canterbury with two round drum towers projecting from the eastern or outer corners of a square main body. A surviving section of the east wall to the north of the gateway was refaced and given a new parapet in the 14th century when the circular bastion at the NE corner was added. This has a spiral stair and several arrow loops. On the south side the Normans built a new wall a little further out to allow room for the bishop's palace. A new wall further out was built in 1344 but of it only the Prior's Gate still stands. Another wall still further out to the south was erected later in the 14th century, of which long stretches survive on either side of the round SE corner tower.

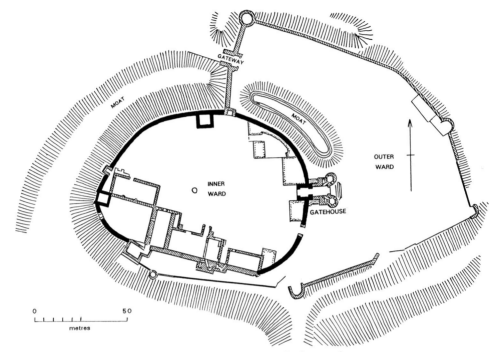

Plan of Saltwood Castle

SALTWOOD CASTLE   TR 161359

Archbishop Lanfranc held Saltwood shortly after the Norman Conquest. It was long associated with the archbishops, but usually occupied by lay tenants. The earthworks of the ringwork and bailey probably go back to when Hugo de Montfort was in possession at the time of Domesday Book. The inner ward walls may be the work of Henry de Essex, Warden of the Cinque Ports. In 1163 de Essex became a monk after being accused of cowardice on the field of battle and Henry II took Saltwood into his own hands despite the claims of de Essex's overlord, Archbishop Thomas Becket. In 1170 the four knights that murdered Becket in Canterbury Cathedral set out from Saltwood, then held by Randolph de Broc, and they returned to it afterwards. The straight south side of the oval inner ward must be a rebuilding after Henry II had the castle slighted following the rebellion of 1173-4, whilst the curtain wall of the outer ward to the east, now broken down to the east and NE, is mostly 14th century.

In the 1380s Archbishop Courtenay (d1401) added a new audience hall and greatly strengthened the gatehouse by adding two lofty round towers to it with four machicolations between them high up. The gatehouse of the outer ward is probably also of this period, together with one round flanking tower. Despite these improvements the castle was said to be in need of repair in 1399. Archbishop Cranmer handed over the castle to Henry VIII in 1540. It was wrecked by an earthquake in the 1580s. In 1885 the Deedes family restored the gatehouse as a residence, adding two wings on the inner side. During the late 20th century Saltwood was the seat of Lord Clarke, writer and presenter of the TV series Civilisation, and his son Allan, the Conservative member of Parliament.

The 6m high curtain wall of the inner ward still stands mostly complete to the wall-walk and parapet and encloses a court 100m long by 65m wide. Projecting entirely internally and contemporary with it are the gatehouse on the east and square towers on the north and west. The towers have pilaster buttresses towards the field. The projecting open-backed turrets close to these towers are probably 13th century additions to provide flanking fire. The two square towers on the south side may also be 13th century. One possibly formed a solar block for the audience hall of the 1380s. This hall was almost entirely rebuilt in the 1930s by Lady Conway but the pointed tunnel-vaulted undercroft with chamfered transverse ribs below it is 14th century work, and so is the east projection containing the access staircase. From the NW corner there was access to a spacious former chapel. Further east is a ruined earlier hall of c1300 reached through a NE porch. Beyond it lies an undercroft over which is another chapel with cusped intersecting tracery in the three-light windows on both sides, those on the south piercing the curtain wall, here well protected by a steep slope to a wide water filled moat held in by a dam on the east. Internally the hoodmoulds form part of a system of wall-arcading.

The lofty towers 7.5m in diameter projecting from the east corners of the late 14th century extension of the inner gatehouse contain vaulted hexagonal guard rooms with shutes behind from the upper storey latrines in rectangular projections. The upper windows, battlements and machicolations were restored in 1885 along with the gateway passage vault.

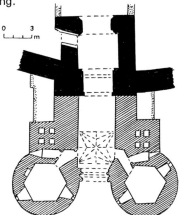

There are round towers with narrow loops at the NW, NE, east and SW corners of the large outer ward, and a square outer gatehouse projects from the west wall, being thus commanded by the inner ward north wall. This ward has its own moat around the NW corner and may be of 13th century origin, although the defences seem mostly 14th century.

Plan of inner gatehouse at Saltwood

Saltwood Castle

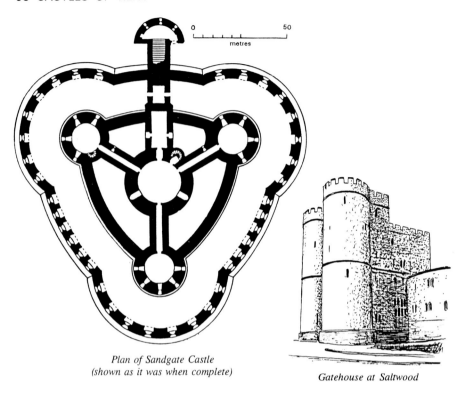

Plan of Sandgate Castle
(shown as it was when complete)

Gatehouse at Saltwood

Chapel at Saltwood Castle

Sandgate Castle

SANDGATE CASTLE   TR 207352   V

This artillery fort was erected on the orders of Henry VIII during the space of 78 weeks from April 1539 to October 1540 to a design by Steffan von Haschenperg. The work was supervised by the first captain, Richard Keys, who had under him a deputy, a porter, five soldiers and eight gunners. In January 1548 the fort was armed with a falcon, a culverin, two sakers, all of brass, and thirteen smaller iron guns, the majority of all these then being broken or dismounted. Shortly after Queen Mary came to the throne in the summer of 1553 the castle was given to Lord Clinton. It was sold to Humphrey Mitchell for £110 in February 1556, only to be sold again in March for 200 marks. In January 1557 the castle was purchased by Edward Watson but it was recovered by the Crown shortly afterwards and in 1558 £45 was spent on replacing timber and lead taken from the building by one of the recent owners. Repairs are also recorded in 1596-9 and in 1644-5, whilst in 1715-16 the central keep was re-roofed and the seaward battery rebuilt after being destroyed by the sea. Apart from this the building retained its 16th century form until 1805-8 when it was remodelled as part of the coastal defences against Napoleon. It was then mostly refaced, adapted to take the new heavier guns, and given bomb-proof vaults of brick. Since then the building has fallen into a ruinous condition, especially on the seaward side, although the central keep remains habitable.

The castle consists of a three storey circular keep 15m in diameter connected at two levels by walls containing passages connecting with rooms in towers 11m in diameter set at the corners of a triangle with curved sides. The spaces between the towers were solid earth at the lower level and open platforms with wide-splayed loops for heavy guns on the upper level. Surrounding the whole building was an outer parapet set on a battered plinth rising from the dry moat. This outer wall had curved sides corresponding to those of the inner wall and half-round bastions around the inner towers. The inner platform facing north to landward was subdivided by a gatehouse built in front of the keep. In front of the gatehouse was a drawbridge over from a passage from a D-shaped barbican which was entered through a doorway in the rear wall facing south, this entrance thus being covered by the main building.

SANDOWN CASTLE   TR 376543

Hardly any traces remain of the northernmost of Henry VIII's three forts guarding the Downs anchorage. It was very similar to Walmer, having four outer bastions and a circular central keep. Along with Deal and Walmer it held a Parliamentary garrison from 1642 until they declared for Charles I in 1648. The defenders harrassed Colonel Rich whilst he was besieging Deal but surrendered soon after Deal was given up. A few years later the guns at Sandown fired on a raider attacking small craft in the Downs. In the 1660s the castle formed the prison of Colonel John Hutchinson, kept here by Charles II for having been a signatory to the execution of Charles I. An engraving of 1735 shows the castle as having survived until then with little alteration. The sea breached the outer wall of the moat in 1785 and the castle was soon declared unfit for habitation, yet it was garrisoned throughout the ·Napoleonic Wars. After being damaged by the sea and a fire the castle was demolished in the late 19th century, some of the materials being re-used at Walmer.

SANDWICH TOWN WALLS   TR 334579   F

Nothing remains of a castle mentioned here in the time of Edward III, who frequently embarked on voyages from here, Sandwich being one of the Cinque Ports. In 1383 the English fleet captured a large French ship carrying a 3,000 foot long prefabricated timber wall 20 feet high with many intermediate turrets able to hold ten men each and it was set up upon the rampart which still encloses the landward sides of the town. The east side of the town, facing the quay, was walled in stone and here lies the Fisher Gate, of stone and flint below with a portcullis groove in the archway, and of yellow brick with red diapering of 1571 above. The gateway called The Barbican has east-facing 16th century bastions with chequerwork and attractive 20th century additions. Sandwich has not much increased in size over the years and the houses do not reach the line of the south and west ramparts. In 1451 the defences were strengthened by the erection of the Great Bulwark in the SE corner of the town. It had two storeys and was armed with cannon. This strongpoint was captured in August 1457 by a French raiding party led by Pierre de Breze, who retired with considerable booty. It was held by Fauconberg for the Earl of Warwick until being demolished by Edward IV after his victory over Warwick at Barnet in 1471.

The Barbican, Sandwich

Scotney Castle

SCOTNEY   TQ 689352   O

In the mid 14th century Scotney passed from the family of that name to Roger Ashburnham. He is said to have built the existing castle about thirty years later but the very irregular layout of the inner ward suggests gradual modifications and additions to an existing building. His son alienated Scotney to Henry Chicheley, Archbishop of Canterbury who used the castle for a while but then in 1418 gave it to his niece Florence on the occasion of her marriage with John Darell. In the 1630s the Darells began an new ashlar-faced mansion fifteen bays long in the middle of the inner ward but lacked sufficient resources to complete it. Part of it was removed when the castle and its surroundings became part of the picturesque prospect from a new house higher up built Anthony Salvin for Edward Hussey in 1837-44.

The castle consists of an inner ward about 55m by 50m and an outer ward about 50m by 35m to the SW, both being islands within a moat forming a lake up to 40m wide on the south side. A causeway on the NW side leads over the moat to the outer ward which may have had a retaining wall and parapet but a no proper curtain wall. The original entrance with a drawbridge lay further west. A bridge on the site of another drawbridge leads to the inner gatehouse in the middle of the SW wall of the inner ward. The lower part of this gatehouse survives, it being about 8m square with diagonal buttresses at all four corners. At each end of this side were corner towers about 8m in diameter, and there were two further towers at the east and north corners. Only foundations remain of three of them but the southern tower rises about 10m from the moat to the top of the machicolated parapet, within which is a 17th century conical roof and lantern. A wing of various dates, including a 16th century window and oriel windows of 1849, joins the tower to the ruins of the classical style 17th century house extending across the court, on the west wall of which is a large boss of c1300 from Bayham Abbey. In the wall between the wing and the ruined house a secret chamber was discovered in 1887, the Darells having remained catholic after the Reformation and in need of a hiding place for their priest, Father Richard Blount. He lived at Scotney from 1591 until betrayed in 1598, although he remained secure in the hiding place whilst the authorities searched the castle for a week.

Fishergate at Sandwich

Town ramparts at Sandwich

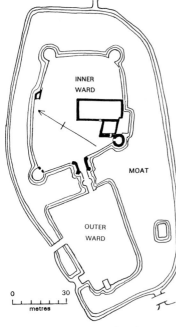

Scotney Castle: site plan

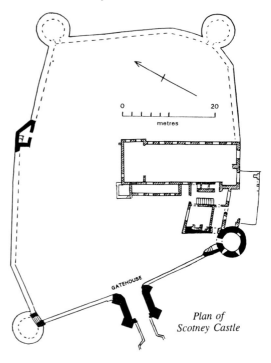

*Plan of
Scotney Castle*

SHOREHAM CASTLE   TQ 525636

A farmhouse with close-set half-timbering of 15th
or 16th century date adjoins on the south side a
fragment of older curtain walling up to 1.8m thick
which revetted a knoll set in a swampy valley.

SHURLAND HOUSE   TQ 994716

The large ruined early 16th century house, presumed to have been completed prior
to a visit by Henry VIII in 1536, lies on or near the site of an older moated house. The
ruin is of brick with stone dressings and has two octagonal turrets dividing the west
facade into three parts, with a gateway in the middle. The north and south ranges are
very damaged and the only remains of the east range are the base of its inner wall.

SISSINGHURST CASTLE   TQ 809384   O

Only the east and north arms of the wet moat survive of the house of the de Berham family in which Edward I stayed for four nights in 1305. There is no evidence of stone defences of that period. In the 1490s Sissinghurst was sold to the Baker family of Cranbrook and they built a new mansion outside the west arm of the moat. Only the entrance range of this remains, with a gatehouse inserted by Sir John Baker in the 1530s. He became Attorney General, Chancellor of the Exchequer, and Speaker of the House of Commons, and died in 1558, aged 70. In the 1560s his son Sir Richard Baker demolished most of the late 15th century house and built a new mansion with a courtyard across where the western arm of the medieval moat must have been. Of this house, in which Elizabeth I was entertained 1573, there remains only the brick four storey gatehouse flanked by octagonal turrets in the centre of the west range and a fragment of the private rooms in the SE corner made into a cottage.

The Elizabethan house was left to decay after the Civil War. The place was further damaged, especially internally, when it was leased to the government for use as a prison for French seamen captured during the Seven Years War which ended in 1763. Only from this period onwards was the unfortified building referred to as a castle. One of the officers then serving here was Edward Gibbon, who later wrote "The Decline and Fall of the Roman Empire". Most of the house was demolished c1800 by Sir Horace Mann, whose uncle purchased the estate in 1764. The present fame of Sissinghurst is mostly because of the very fine gardens created by Vita Sackville-West and her husband Sir Harold Nicholson, who purchased the estate in 1930.

STAPLEHURST   TQ 784407

On the north side of a stream lies a small ringwork surrounded by a wet moat.

STOCKBURY   TQ 846617

The northern part of a ditched ringwork about 40m across has been destroyed. To the east, towards the parish church, lie two sections of rampart of a crescent shaped bailey 35m wide and 85m long.

STONE   TQ 584740

At the SE tower of the Tudor-style house mostly of the 1820s is a square tower of flint 12m high with two narrow loops facing north. It could be of almost any medieval date. In the 14th century Stone was occupied by the Northwold family. A later occupant was Sir John Wiltshire, Comptroller of Calais, d1526, whose monument lies in the nearby parish church.

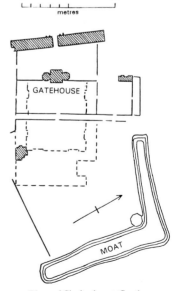

Plan of Sissinghurst Castle

STOWTING CASTLE   TR 123420

On level ground beside a stream west of the church are a worn motte and bailey.

SUTTON VALENCE CASTLE   TQ 816491   F

On top of a south-facing escarpment overlooking the Weald are ruins of a keep 11.6m square over ragstone walls up to 2.5m thick with clasping corner buttresses. Ragged holes mark the positions of basement loops facing east, west and south and there was a spiral stair in the NE corner and a wall-chamber at second storey level in the SW corner, but little remains of the upper parts. A square forebuilding lay against the north side. Of the bailey there are slight traces of a curtain wall built on a natural cliff face on the west, and a century ago there were said to be traces of a tower on the east.

The Valence part of the name refers to the family that held the castle for three generations after Henry III gave Sutton to his half-brother William de Valance, later Earl of Pembroke. The keep, however, looks like work of the second half of the 12th century. The castle later passed to the Cliffords and then to the Harpers, before being sold to Sir Edward Hales. The remains were excavated in 1956 and are now maintained by English Heritage.

Sutton Valence Castle

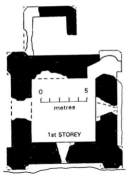

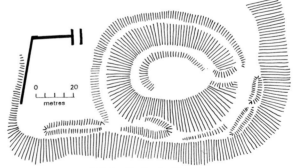

Plan of keep, Sutton Valence

Plan of Godard's Castle, Thurnham

SWANSCOMBE RINGWORK   TQ 603735

A ringwork 30m across with a rampart rising 2.5m above its ditch was destroyed in 1928 and there is now nothing to see.

THURNHAM CASTLE   TQ 808581

Set side by side on a south facing promontory are a motte and bailey, now both very overgrown. Around the north and west sides of the bailey are remains of a flint curtain wall with the lower part of a gatehouse on the north side. Also known as Godard's Castle, this fortress belonged to the de Says and then the de Thurnhams. A charter of c1215-19 mentions land within the walls of the castle.

Remains of curtain wall, Godard's Castle, Thurnham

TONBRIDGE CASTLE   TQ 589466   O

This castle was founded by Richard Fitzgilbert after he was given an estate here by William I. He was subsequently known as Richard de Clare from the estate of that name he held in Suffolk with castle earthworks similar to those of Tonbridge. Richard and his son joined in the 1088 rebellion of Bishop Odo against William II. The king besieged Tonbridge and the castle was surrendered after Richard was wounded. He subsequently retired to a monastery. Archbishop Thomas Becket in Henry II's reign argued that Tonbridge was originally a property belonging to his archbishopric and tried to make Roger de Clare, second Earl of Hertford, do homage to him for it, but without success. Roger is said to have made Thomas's messenger eat his summoning charter, wax seals and all. The castle was captured by King John in 1215 but was returned to the de Clares by Henry III. After Richard de Clare succeeded as a minor in 1230 Archbishop Wethershed made another claim upon Tonbridge. He went off to Rome and gained the support of the Pope but died during the return journey.

Gilbert de Clare, known as the Red Earl, supported Simon de Montfort against Henry III in 1264 and in consequence the castle was captured by the royalist forces, the town being burnt and Countess Alice being taken prisoner. Earl Gilbert changed sides in 1265 and supported Prince Edward when the latter defeated de Montfort at Evesham. Shortly afterwards he began one of Britain's mightiest castles, Caerphilly in Glamorgan, in defiance of Llywelyn ap Gruffydd. The east gatehouse of the inner ward at Caerphilly is very similar in layout to that at Tonbridge. Unfortunately we cannot be sure of the exact date of either gatehouse but the most likely scenario seems to be that at Caerphilly was begun c1271-2 and that at Tonbridge c1280, i.e. after Edward I was sumptuously entertained at Tonbridge in 1274.

Gatehouse at Tonbridge

Interior of Gatehouse at Tonbridge

Curtain wall at Tonbridge

After the last of the de Clares, another Gilbert, was killed fighting the Scots at Bannockburn in 1314, Tonbridge passed to his sister Eleanor, who was soon married off to the hated favourite Hugh le Despenser. Edward II was forced to banish the Despensers in 1321 and Tonbridge then went to Hugh d'Audley. He in turn lost possession after supporting the Earl of Lancaster's rebellion in 1322 but subsequently got it back. On his death Tonbridge passed to his son-in-law Ralph, Lord Stafford. He is said to have added two towers to the bailey curtain wall, the Stafford Tower and the Water Tower. Henry Stafford, Duke of Buckingham, was executed by Richard III and the family finally lost Tonbridge after his son Edward was executed in 1520 by Henry VIII. In 1643 the castle was garrisoned by Parliament. A Royalist force advanced into the town in June but was defeated and the castle remained untaken, although the gardens of the tenant Thomas Weller were wrecked by the defenders. In 1646 the defences were ordered to be slighted and the curtain wall seems to have then been breached although the stonework of the gatehouse remains almost intact. Stone is said to have been taken from the walls to build locks to make the Medway navigable in the mid 18th century. The house east of the gatehouse was completed in 1792 by Thomas Hooker, only to be sold a year later to William Woodgate. The last owner occupant was William Bailey. He bequeathed it to the trustees for Frances, Lady Stafford. The castle was then let out for use firstly as a home, then a military academy in the 1860s, and then a boys prep school. In 1897 the trustees sold it to Tonbridge Urban District Council which used the house as offices and opened the grounds as a public park.

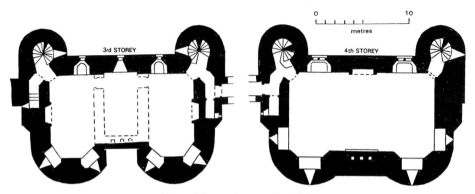

Plans of the gatehouse at Tonbridge

The lozenge-shaped inner bailey lies above the north bank of the River Medway and measures about 100m east-west by 70m wide. To the north lay an outer bailey probably never defended in stone, and beyond to the north and east was the town, defended by a ditch. Of the bailey curtain wall 2.7m thick probably of 12th century date there remains the entire south side in a somewhat mutilated state with several buttresses, latrine shafts and a postern, plus a fragment of the east side and the wall running west from the gatehouse up the motte to the keep. The latter retains part of a wall-walk with the traces of parapets on each side. Not much remains of the two towers at the bailey southern corners. A modern zig-zag path leads up the motte to the last traces of a shell keep with a maximum diameter of about 20m within a retaining wall which seems to have been only about 1m thick. The stepped plinth and buttresses facing SE towards the bailey are later additions. Still surrounding the north and west sides of the motte base is a water-filled moat which presumably once extended along the north side of the inner bailey.

The twin-round towered gatehouse is described in a 1521 survey of the forfeited Stafford estates "as strong a fortress as few be in England". It is faced with yellow ashlar and has four surviving levels, the lowest of which were lightless store-rooms below ground level. At ground level there is a central gateway passage flanked by guard rooms, that on the west having a latrine in a projection. The guardrooms have loops with bottom roundels commanding the field and the passage, off which they were reached by doorways with portcullises. The passage was commanded by murder holes in the vault and closed by portcullises both north and south of the guardroom doorways, so that the gatehouse could be defended against both the outer and inner baileys as a self-contained citadel. From the guardrooms spiral stairs rise up in round turrets at the SW and SE corners. These turrets have spurred bases like those of the main towers. On the next level the towers contained private chambers each with two loops towards the field, a single-light window with seats in the embrasure towards the inner bailey, and fireplaces in the side walls with latrines behind them. These chambers flanked a room from which three of the portcullises were operated. The main outer portcullis was operated from the fourth level, which was a hall or state chamber with two light windows in the south wall with the portcullis between them and a latrine on the east opening off where the curtain wall walk led off. The wall-walk on the west lay at the level of the chambers. Both these doorway to the wall-walks were closed by portcullises. The top of the building is somewhat damaged but the base of one loop of the parapet remains visible on the south side.

The shell keep, Tonbridge

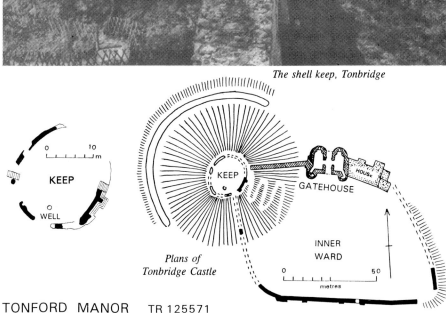

*Plans of
Tonbridge Castle*

TONFORD MANOR   TR 125571

The 18th century house the hall of the house which Sir Thomas Browne, Treasurer to Henry VI, was licensed to crenellate in 1449, with one six-light window in the outer wall. The NW front has the remains of four circular turrets with intermediate buttresses, two of which contain latrines. The inner lining of the walls is of brick. Closeby, near a corner of the enciente, is a projecting gatehouse of two storeys with semicircular responds to the four-centred arch. Part of the moat remains on the SE.

TONGE CASTLE   TQ 933636

A ditch 15m wide protects the NE and NW sides of a platform now protected on the SE and SW by a mill pond. The enclosure is roughly 70m square but is much mutilated and it is not clear what the original layout of the earthwork was. Excavations revealed thin foundations and pottery from the 12th century to the 14th century. Tonge belonged to the Mortimers and later reverted to the Crown.

UPNOR CASTLE   TQ 758707   E

In 1559 Elizabeth I purchased six acres of land on the north bank of the Medway for the construction of a bulwark or artillery fort to guard naval ships at anchor further up the estuary. Sir Richard Lee drew up a plan for the fort but he was preoccupied with the job of building the impressive defences of Berwick-upon-Tweed and the work at Upnor was overseen by his deputy Humphrey Locke, whilst the site management and accounts were left to Richard Watts of Rochester. His accounts for the period 1559 to 1564 survive and record expenditure of £3621. Stone was brought from demolished buildings at Rochester Castle. The Queen was evidently not satisfied with the rate of progress and early in 1561 wrote to the Lord Admiral demanding completion of the work. A further £728 was spent on completing the building in 1567, a third of this going on lead for the roof. A chain was later put across the Medway close to the castle (it was later moved downstream), maintenance of it in 1588 being £80. The castle garrison then included six gunners under a master gunner. In 1596 Admiral Howard reported that the castle was inadequately manned and in consequence the garrison was increased to eighty men.

In 1599-1601 over £1100 was spent on improvements, a ditch being provided on the landward side and a timber palisade being built in front of the bastion towards the river. In 1603 the guns at Upnor comprised a demi-cannon, seven culverin, five demi-culverin, a minion, a falcon, a saker and four fowlers each with two chambers. Two outworks, Warham Sconce and Bay Sconce, each had two culverin with four or five demi-culverin. In 1623 there were eighteen guns at Upnor and the unserviceable equipment included 34 longbows. The garrison then comprised a captain, a master gunner, seven gunners and twenty soldiers. The place was then somewhat decayed and the drawbridge and its raising machinery were broken.

During the Civil War the castle was held for Parliament and used to incarcerate Royalist officers. The castle was briefly held by the Royalists during the uprising of 1648. In 1650 a warrant was issued for reimbursing Major Brown, the Parliamentary commander, for repairs costing £673. This work seems to have included the heightening of the gatehouse after it was damaged by fire, and about this time the open backs of the north and south towers were closed off.

Gatehouse at Upnor Castle

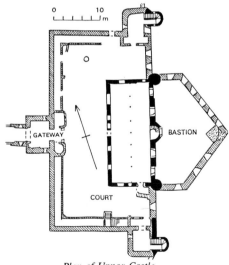

Plan of Upnor Castle

In 1667 a Dutch fleet under Admiral de Ruyter managed to capture and destroy naval ships in the estuary, the very thing the castle was built to prevent. The chain proved no obstacle despite batteries being quickly set up at each end of it. The castle seems to have been seriously short of munitions although the garrison did their best to keep up a heavy fire on the Dutch fleet. New forts at Gillingham and at Cockham Wood were built in 1669 to supplement the Medway defences. Slight traces of the latter, 2km east of Upnor, still survive. Upnor then no longer constituted the first line of defence and became "a Place of Stores and Magazine". In 1691 the stores at Upnor included 164 iron guns with carriages, 7125 round shot, 204 muskets, 77 pikes and 5206 barrels of gunpowder. A barracks was built to the SW c1720. Upnor was last used as a magazine in 1827 and then became an Ordnance Laboratory. It continued in military use until in 1961 it became a national monument open to the public. It is now administered by English Heritage.

The castle consists of a block 22m long by 11m wide standing on the seaward side of a court 35m long by 20m wide defended by a low wall and a ditch and containing a well. In front of the main building lies an angular bastion on which were mounted heavy guns looking out to sea. In front of this bastion is a wooden palisade to keep ships from coming right up alongside. The bastion is part of the original building of 1559 but the parapet is of 1599. The main building is of 1559 and contains passages at the lowest level, then two levels of what were originally barrack rooms but later used to contain powder barrels, to take the weight of which the floors had to be re-enforced. The top part of the building is late 17th century. Quite how this building was originally defended to landward is uncertain since the present defences are of 1599-1601 and later. The north and south towers flanking shore and the adjacent walls of the court are of 1599, but incorporating half-round stair turrets of 1559 with key-hole pistol loops on the seaward side and with later walls closing off their interiors when they were given an extra third storey. The upper parts of the south tower are reached by an external staircase. Together with the main building they make quite an impressive front towards the sea. In the middle of the west wall of the court is a square gatehouse of 1599 with a 17th century barbican in front. Towards the court the gatehouse has two square turrets with round corners. One of them contains a spiral stair to two upper storeys and a gun-platform on top. The brick upper parts of the building are of the 1650s. The ditch was originally deeper and was covered by double-splayed gunports in the gatehouse and north and south towers.

Old print of Upnor Castle

Gateway at Upnor

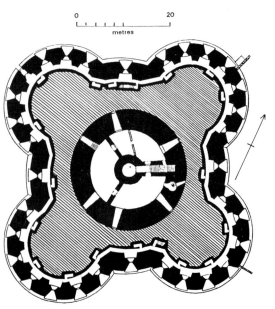

Plan of Walmer Castle

WALMER CASTLE   TR 378501   E

Walmer is the southernmost of three forts begun in 1539 by Henry VIII to guard the anchorage of the Downs, and was probably completed in 1540, when it was garrisoned by a captain, deputy, a porter and eleven gunners. In 1648 the Parliamentary garrison at Walmer went over to the cause of King Charles and was besieged by Colonel Rich. It took a week before the attackers were sent a mortar and when it arrived there was no engineer with it. They were also harrased by attacks from landing parties from the fleet and from the garrisons at Deal and Sandown. The defenders surrendered after three weeks when it became clear they would not be relieved. The castle was repaired and kept garrisoned and in 1661, after the restoration of Charles II, it had sixteen gunners. In 1708 the castle became the residence of the Duke of Dorset in his capacity of Lord Warden of the Cinque Ports. He added extra rooms out onto the bastions from the keep. William Pitt held the office in 1792-1806 and it was later held by the Duke of Wellington, who died at Walmer in 1852. Lord Granville added thirteen rooms above the gatehouse soon after taking office as Lord Warden in 1865. The castle was visited by Princess Victoria in 1835 and in 1842 as queen she returned to stay a month with Prince Albert and their two eldest children. Personal effects of these 19th century wardens and their visitors were carefully preserved on the orders of Lord Granville's successor, W.H.Smith (of book selling fame), installed in 1891. Another notable Lord Warden, Sir Winston Churchill, appointed in 1946, never took up residence at Walmer. The castle has been in state care as a monument since 1904 and is now maintained by English Heritage. A flat in the castle is still available for the use of the present Lord Warden.

Walmer Castle

Walmer is a smaller and simplified version of Deal. Here the central keep 25m in external diameter has no flanking bastions and there are only four on the outer circuit. As at Deal the entrance is in the outer part of one bastion, a later bridge reaching out across the dry moat to meet it. Covering this moat is a lower level of ports for handguns opening off a passage running round the whole of the outer walls and reached by stairs from the court on the north and south sides. The central keep was arranged as at Deal with three rib-vaulted cellars surrounding a central well, then barrack rooms above and officers' rooms on top, but the upper levels have been much altered and there is a north extension of c1730 containing a dining room and drawing room. Two rooms in the keep were occupied by Queen Victoria and Prince Albert in 1842. Another is known as William Pitt's Room. The upper parts of the outer bastions have also been modified. Only the south bastion now retains thick walls pierced by widely splayed gunports at courtyard level. These ports now serve windows for rooms built within the bastion, one of these being that in which the Duke of Wellington lived and died.

Walmer Castle

Westenhanger Castle

WESTENHANGER CASTLE   TR 123372

John de Kiriel was licensed by Edward III to fortify his house here in 1343. The accommodation was improved during Henry VIII's reign by Sir Edward Poynings, Lord Deputy of Ireland. It was later held by Sir Thomas Smythe but during a visit to this district Elizabeth I gave Westenhanger to Sir Thomas Sackville. After the failure of the Royalist rising of 1648 prisoners were kept in the castle. In 1701 most of the building was demolished for the value of the materials and a farmhouse was built in the NE corner. In the late 18th century this was replaced by the present two storey house, restored a few years ago. It lies on flat ground just west of Folkestone Racecourse.

A wet moat, now dry, enclosed a wall about 1.3m thick around a court of irregular plan but roughly a square of 55m. Not much of it remains on the south side but it still stands on the other sides, even if mostly reduced in height and fragmentary in places. At the SE corner is the base of a tower about 6m square projecting diagonally and there were similar towers set in the middle of each side, except on the west, where the gateway was situated. The north mid-wall tower stands almost complete. The inner parts of the bases remain of round towers about 6m in diameter at the SW and NW corners, whilst the larger Rosamund's Tower adjoining the house at the NE corner stands 12m high to the eaves of a conical cap. The name is said to refer to Rosamund Clifford, mistress of Henry II, although she lived nearly two centuries earlier than the mid 14th century. The farmhouse is built against the old outer wall, which here has a six-light early 16th century window high up. The hall (reported to be 15m long by 9.5m wide) and principal private rooms, plus a 16th century vaulted chapel 10m by 5m, lay on this side. Parts remain of the western range, including the walls which flanked the gateway passage, with four pairs of half-octagonal responds for the ribs of a vault. An old plan shows polygonal stair turrets towards the court in the SW and NW corners and in the middle of the south side, but nothing now remains of these 16th century additions. There was probably an outer court to the west where there are two large stone 16th century barns at right-angles to each other.

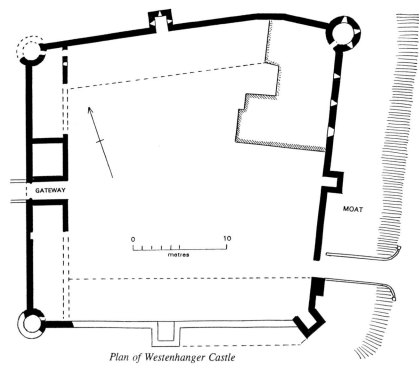

GATEWAY

0   10
metres

MOAT

Plan of Westenhanger Castle

Westenhanger Castle

Old print of Westenhanger Castle

Westenhanger Castle

Westenhanger Castle

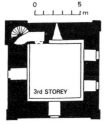

West Malling: plan of tower

St Leonard's Tower, West Malling

WEST MALLING   TQ 676571   E

This 18m high tower is generally thought to have been built by Gundulph, Bishop of Rochester in the 1090s. It is called St Leonard's Tower as if it were part of a church, and it seems there was a chapel closeby at one time, yet although it lacks either fireplaces or latrines the tower is thought to have been a solar tower or keep, presumably once accompanied by other domestic buildings either of stone or wood. The tower stands on a rock outcrop and measures 10m square over walls 2.4m thick above the plinth. There are small clasping buttresses on three of the corners, and a rather larger one at the NW corner, which contains a spiral stair. The doorway at the foot of this stair seems to have been broken through later and the original entrance is thought to have been at this level in the east wall, where there is an internal recess. The south face has a pilaster buttress in the middle. On this side and on the east there is blind arcading at second storey level. This level has centrally placed loops facing north, east and west but no communication with the staircase. The top storey has two large round headed windows facing east and a single opening in each of the other sides. Over the years the tower has seen use as a prison and hop store. It belonged to the Rainey family in the 17th century and was sold by them to the Honywoods. It is now in the care of English Heritage.

GLOSSARY OF TERMS

ASHLAR - Masonry of blocks with even faces and square edges. BAILEY - Defensible court enclosed by a wall or a palisade and ditch. BARBICAN - Defensible court, passage or porch in front of an entrance. BASTION - A projection rising no higher than the curtain wall. BLOCKHOUSE - A free-standing tower or similar building designed to mount cannon. CAPONIER - A vaulted passage projecting out into a ditch with loops to cover it with flanking fire. CRENEL - A cut-away part of a parapet. CORBEL - A projecting bracket to support other stonework or a timber beam. CURTAIN WALL - A high enclosing stone wall around a bailey. DEMI-BASTION - Bastion flanking just one side of the enceinte instead of two. EMBATTLED - Provided with a a parapet with indentations (crenellations). FOUR-CENTRED ARCH - An arch drawn with four compass points, two on each side. GUNPORT - an embrasure suitable for the discharge of heavy cannon. JAMB - A side of a doorway, window or other opening. KEEP - A citadel or ultimate strongpoint. The term is not medieval and such towers were then called donjons, from which word is derived the word dungeon meaning a prison. LIGHT - A compartment of a window. LOOP - A small opening to admit light or for the discharge of missiles. MACHICOLATION - A slot for dropping or firing missiles at assailants. MERLONS - The upstanding portions of a parapet. MOAT - A defensive ditch, water filled or dry. MOTTE - A steep sided flat-topped mound, partly or wholly man-made. OILLET - Small circular hole. PARAPET - A wall for protection at any sudden drop. PLINTH - The projecting base of a wall. It may be battered (sloped) or stepped. PORTCULLIS - A wooden gate made to rise and fall in vertical grooves, being hoisted by a windlass above. POSTERN - A back entrance or lesser gateway. RINGWORK - An embanked enclosure of more modest size than a bailey, generally of greater width but less elevated than a motte summit. SHELL KEEP - A small stone walled court built upon a motte or ringwork. SOLAR - A private living room for the lord and his family. STRONGHOUSE - A mansion not easy to break into or burn down because of its solid walls and moat but not provided with battlements or loopholes for an active defence. TOWER HOUSE - Self contained defensible house with the main rooms stacked vertically. WALL-WALK - A walkway on top of a wall, always protected by a parapet. WARD - A stone walled defensive enclosure.

PUBLIC ACCESS TO THE SITES   Codes used in the gazetteers.

E Buildings in the care of English Heritage. Fee payable at some sites.
F Sites to which there is free access at any time.
H Buildings currently used as hotels, restaurants, shops (free access to outside).
O Buildings opened to the public by private owners, local councils, National Trust.
V Buildings closely visible from public roads, paths, churchyards & open spaces.

FURTHER READING

The Buildings of North East and East Kent, John Newman, 1969
The Buildings of West Kent and The Weald, John Newman, 1969
The Victoria County History of Kent, several volumes, various dates.
A History of the King's Works, several volumes, 1963-70
Norman Castles in Britain, Derek Renn, 1968
Castellarium Anglicanum, D.Cathcart King, 1983
Pamphlet guides are available for Deal, Dover, Eynsford, Hever, Leeds, Penshurst,
    Rochester, Scotney, Sissinghurst, Tonbridge, Upnor and Walmer
See also periodicals such as Fortress, Medieval Archeology, Archeological Journal
    and Country Life.